I0120244

John Sweney

Redemption songs

John Sweney

Redemption songs

ISBN/EAN: 9783337266349

Printed in Europe, USA, Canada, Australia, Japan

Cover: Foto ©Thomas Meinert / pixelio.de

More available books at **www.hansebooks.com**

REDEMPTION SONGS:

MUSICAL EDITORS:

JNO. R. SWENEY, WM. J. KIRKPATRICK
AND JNO. J. LOWE.

Philadelphia: JOHN J. HOOD, 1018 Arch St.

Copyright, 1889, by JOHN J. HOOD.

Price, 35 cents per copy, by mail, prepaid; $3.60 per dozen, not prepaid.

COPYRIGHT, 1889, BY JOHN J. HOOD.

PREFACE.

I believe this volume of songs will meet any demand **for devotional and** evangelistic meetings. I believe this because of the following reasons :—

First—The ability of the editors.

Second—The large number of contributors; embracing almost every prominent writer of Gospel songs of the past twenty five years. Here are their names :—

LOWRY,	TOWNER,	DUNBAR,	HARTSOUGH,
DOANE,	STEBBINS,	STOCKTON,	DAVIS.
BLISS	PALMER,	PERKINS,	WILLIAMS,
SANKEY,	KNAPP,	KANE,	NICKERSON,
ROOT,	EXCELL,	MINOR,	OGDEN,
BRADBURY,	McINTOSH,	HASTY,	GORDON,
O'KANE,	LORENZ,	HOFFMAN,	SMITH.
MASON,	BILHORN,	TOMER,	
McGRANAHAN,	CONVERSE,	BUTLER,	

Third—It contains the largest and best collection of first-class devotional hymns of any single collection I have ever seen.

Fourth—I have tested nearly all the pieces in this book, and found them to be both popular and effective.

Thanks are due all contributors and owners of copyrights, who have by their kindness enabled me to compile this volume, and are hereby offered.

PROPERTY NOTICE:

To PRINT, for sale or otherwise, any copyright hymn of this collection, unless written permission shall have b en obtained, will be deemed an infringement of copyright.

REDEMPTION SONGS.

By Grace I Will.

E. E. Hewitt.   Wm. J. Kirkpatrick.

1. { Will you go to Je - sus now, dear friend? He is calling you to-day;
   { Will you seek the bright and better land, By" the true and living way?

2. { Would you know the Saviour's boundless love, And his mercy rich and free?
   { Will you seek the saving, cleansing blood, That was shed for you and me.

REFRAIN.

I will, I will! by the grace of God, I will; I will go to Jesus now; I will

heed the gospel call. For the promise is for all; I will go to Je- sus now.

3 Will you consecrate your life to him,
   To be ever his alone?
And your loving service freely yield,
   To the King upon his throne.

4 Will you follow where the Master
   Choosing only his renown,   [leads,
Will you daily bear the cross for him,
   Till he bids you wear the crown?

Copyright, 1889, by Wm. J. Kirkpatrick.

4

O Blessed Word.

L. W. MUNHALL.

JNO. R. SWENEY.

1. E-ter-nal life is in God's Word For dead and dy-ing men;
2. God's strength is in his Ho-ly Word; We need it ev-'ry day:
3. By this same Word we know our task, And how it should be done;

By it a-lone we know the Lord, Un-seen by mor-tal ken.
In all our con-flicts this the sword Our spir-it foes to slay.
How now to live, and how at last Our crown is to be won.

CHORUS.

O bless-ed Word, . . . O gracious Word, ... We'll
love . . . thee more and more; . . Be thou our Life, our Strength, our

love thee more and more, We'll love thee more and more; Be thou our Life,

Sword . . . 'Till earth - - - ly strife is o'er. . . . .
our Strength, our Sword 'Till earth-ly strife is o'er, 'Till earth-ly strife is o'er.

rit.

Copyright, 1880, by Jno. R. Sweney.

I will Sing the Wondrous Story.

"I will sing of the mercies of the Lord forever."
Ps. i 89.

H. RAWLEY.   P. BILHORN.

1. I will sing the wond'rous sto-ry, Of the Christ who died for me,
2. I was lost, but Je-sus found me, Found the sheep that went astray;
3. I was bruised, but Jesus healed me, Faint was I from ma-ny-a fall,

How he left his home in glo-ry, For the cross on Cal-va-ry.
Threw his lov-ing arms around me, Drew me back in-to his way.
Sight was gone, and fears possessed me, But he freed me from them all.

CHORUS.

Yes, I'll sing the wondrous sto-ry Of the Christ who died for
Yes, I'll sing   the wondrous story,   Of the Christ

me, ... Sing it with . . . the saints in glo- -ry, Gathered
who died for me,   Sing it with   the saints in glo-ry,

by . . . the crystal sea.
Gathered by   the crystal sea.

4 Days of darkness still come o'er
   Sorrow's path I often tread,
   But the Saviour still is with me
   By his hand I'm safely led.

5 He will keep me till the river
   Rolls its waters at my feet;
   Then he'll bear me safely over,
   Where the loved ones I shall meet.

By permission of Ira D. Sankey, owner of copyright.

Some Sweet Day.

Arthur W. French.   " The hour is coming."--John v. 28.   D. B. Towner.   By per.

Moderato.

1. We shall reach the riv - er side Some sweet day, some sweet day;
2. We shall pass in - side the gate Some sweet day, some sweet day;
3. We shall meet our loved and own Some sweet day, some sweet day;

We shall cross the storm - y tide Some sweet day, some sweet day;
Peace and plen - ty for us wait Some sweet day, some sweet day;
Gath'ring round the great white throne Some sweet day, some sweet day;

We shall press the sands of gold, While be - fore our eyes un - fold
We shall hear the wondrous strain, Glo - ry to the Lamb that's slain,
By the tree of life so fair, Joy and rap - ture ev - 'rywhere,

Heav-en's splendors, yet un - told, Some sweet day, some sweet day.
Christ was dead, but lives a - gain, Some sweet day, some sweet day.
O the bliss of o - ver there! Some sweet day, some sweet day.

Look and Live.

W. A. O.

W. A. OGDEN.

1. I've a mes-sage from the Lord, Hal-le-lu-jah! The
2. I've a mes-sage full of love, Hal-le-lu-jah! A
3. Life is of-fered un-to thee, Hal-le-lu-jah! E-
4. I will tell you how I came, Hal-le-lu-jah! To

mes-sage un-to you I'll give, 'Tis re-cord-ed in his word,
mes-sage, oh! my friend, for you, 'Tis a mes-sage from a-bove,
ter-nal life thy soul shall have, If you'll on-ly look to him,
Je-sus, when he made me whole; 'Twas be-liev-ing on his name,

D.S.—'Tis re-cord-ed in his word,

Fine.

Hal-le-lu-jah! It is on-ly that you "look and live."
Hal-le-lu-jah! Je-sus said it, and I know 'tis true.
Hal-le-lu-jah! Look to Je-sus who a-lone can save.
Hal-le-lu-jah! I trust-ed and he saved my soul.

Hal-le-lu-jah! It is on-ly that you "look and live."

CHORUS.

D.S.

Look and live, . . . my brother, live, Look to Je-sus now and live:

look and live, look and live,

Copyright, 1887, by E. O. Excell.

The True Shepherd.

F. W. Faber

Wm. J. Kirkpatrick.

1. I was wan-der-ing and wea-ry When my Saviour came un-to me;
2. At first I would not hearken, And put off till the morrow;
3. At last I stopped to list-en, His voice could not deceive me:
4. He took me on his shoulder, And ten-der-ly he kissed me;

For the ways of sin grew dreary, And the world had ceased to woo me: And I
But life be-gan to dark-en, And I was sick with sorrow; Still I
I saw his kind eyes glisten, So anxious to relieve me. I was
He bade my love be bold-er, And said how he had missed me; Then I

CHORUS.

thought I heard him say, As he came along his way, O wand'ring souls,
thought I heard him say, As he came along his way, come near me,
sure I heard him say, As he came along his way,
heard him sweetly say, As he went along his way,

rit. ad lib.

My sheep should never fear me,
My sheep should never fear me: I am the Shepherd true.

5 I thought his love would weaken,
As more and more he knew me;
But it burneth like a beacon,
And its light and heat go thro' me.
And I ever hear him say,
As he goes along his way,

6 Let us do, then, dearest brothers, [us.
What will best and longest please
Follow not the ways of others,
But trust ourselves to Jesus.
We shall ever hear him say,
As he goes along his way,

Copyright, 1868, by Wm. J. Kirkpatrick.

Standing on the Promises.

R. K. C.

R. KELSO CARTER.

1. Standing on the prom-is - es of Christ my King, Thro' e - ter - nal
2. Standing on the prom-is - es that can - not fail, When the howling
3. Standing on the prom-is - es I now can see Per - fect, present
4. Standing on the prom-is - es of Christ the Lord, Bound to him e -
5. Standing on the prom-is - es I can - not fall, Listening ev - ery

a - ges let his prais-es ring; Glo-ry in the highest, I will shout and sing,
storms of doubt and fear as-sail, By the liv - ing Word of God I shall pre - vail,
cleansing in the blood for me; Standing in the liberty where Christ makes free,
ter - nally by love's strong cord, O - vercoming dai - ly with the Spir-its' sword,
moment to the Spir-its' call, Rest-ing in my Saviour, as my all in all,

CHORUS.

Standing on the promises of God. Stand - ing, stand - ing,
Standing on the promises, Standing on the promises,

Standing on the promis- es of God my Saviour; Stand - - ing,
Standing on the promis- es,

stand - - ing, I'm standing on the promis- es of God.
Standing on the prom- is- es,

Copyright, 1886, by John J. Hood.

From " Songs of Perfect Love," by per.

Glory to God, Hallelujah!

FANNY J. CROSBY.   WM. J. KIRKPATRICK.

1. We are nev-er, nev-er wea-ry of the grand old song; Glo-ry to
2. We are lost a-mid the rapture of redeem-ing love; Glo-ry to
3. We are go-ing to a palace that is built of gold; Glo-ry to
4. There we'll shout redeeming mercy in a glad, new song; Glo-ry to

God, hal-le-lu-jah! We can sing it loud as ever, with our faith more strong.
God, hal-le-la-jah! We are rising on its pinions to the hills a-bove:
God, hal-le-lujah! Where the King in all his splendor we shall soon behold:
God, hallelujah! There we'll sing the praise of Jesus with the blood-wash'd throng:

Fine. CHORUS.

Glo-ry to God, hal-le-lu-jah! O, the children of the Lord have a

right to shout and sing, For the way is grow-ing bright, and our

D. S.

souls are on the wing: We are going by and by to the palace of a King!

Copyright, 1885, by Wm. J. Kirkpatrick.

Good News.

E. E. HEWITT. Jno. R. Sweney.

1. Good news! good news of a soul redeemed, A pen - i- tent for- giv - en! Good
2. Good news! good news that another heart Has learned redemption's story; Good
3. Good news! good news that another life Will show the power of Je - sus, Will
4. Good news! good news that another hand Will precious seed be sow- ing, An-

news! good news that an - oth - er friend is on the way to heav · en!
news! good news that an - oth - er voice will sing his praise in glo - ry.
prove the might of the sav - ing grace Which daily, hour- ly frees us.
oth - er guide to lead straying feet Where living streams are flowing.

CHORUS.

Rejoice! rejoice! there's joy to-day In the land beyond the riv- er; An-

oth - er gem for His di - a - dem, A star to shine for - ev - er.

Copyright, 1888, by Jno. R. Sweney.

Showers of Blessing.

"And I will cause the shower to come down in his season."
Ezekiel xxxiv. 26.

Annie Garrett.

Jno. R. Sweney.

1. Here in thy name we are gathered, Come and revive us, O Lord
2. O that the showers of bless-ing Now on our souls may descend.
3. There shall be showers of blessing,—Promise that never can fail;
4. Showers of blessing,—we need them, Showers of blessing from thee;

"There shall be showers of bless-ing" Thou hast declared in thy word.
While at the footstool of mer - cy Pleading thy promise we bend!
Thou wilt regard our pe - ti - tion; Sure-ly our faith will pre-vail.
Showers of blessing,—oh, grant them; Thine all the glory shall be.

CHORUS.

Oh, gracious-ly hear us, Gracious-ly hear us, we pray:

gracious-ly hear us,

Pour from thy windows upon us Showers of blessing to - day.

Lord, pour up - on us

Copyright, 1868, by Jno. R. Sweney.

Go On!

GEO. K. THOMPSON.   WM. J. KIRKPATRICK.

1. Go on, ye soldiers of the cross, With courage bold and dar-ing,
2. Though dangers lie on ev-'ry side, And coming storms a-larm us,
3. Go on, go on, and trust in him Whose eye is beaming o'er us,
4. Go on, go on with this our aim, And this our firm en-deav-or,

Go on by faith in Je-sus' name, His roy-al standard bear-ing.
Yet, safe within the Rift-ed Rock, No earthly power can harm us.
Who gives his ho-ly angels charge To guard the way be-fore us.
To gain at last the sun-ny shore And praise our Lord for-ev-er.

CHORUS.

Go on, go on, go on, go on, Proclaim the gos-pel sto-ry!

From step to step, from strength to strength, Go on from grace to glo-ry.

Copyright, 1888, by Wm. J. Kirkpatrick.

Let Him In.

Rev. J. B. Atchinson.

E. O. Excell.

1. There's a stranger at the door, Let him in,
2. O-pen now to him your heart, Let him in,
3. Hear you now his lov-ing voice? Let him in,
4. Now admit the heavenly Guest, Let him in,

Let the Saviour in, let the Saviour in,

He has been there oft be - fore, Let him in;
If you wait he will de - part, Let him in;
Now, oh, now make him your choice, Let him in,
He will make for you a feast, Let him in,

Let the Saviour in, let the Saviour in,

Let him in ere he is gone, Let him in the Ho-ly One,
Let him in, he is your Friend, He your soul will sure de - fend,
He is stand-ing at the door, Joy to you he will re - store,
He will speak your sins for-given, And when earth ties all are riven,

Je-sus Christ, the Father's Son. Let him in.
He will keep you to the end. Let him in.
And his name you will a - dore, Let him in.
He will take you home to heaven, Let him in.

Let the Saviour in. let the Saviour in.

Copyright, 1891, by John J. Hood.

What the Lord has Done for Me.

E. E. Hewitt.　　　　　　　　　　　　　　　　Jno. R. Sweney.

1. Come, dear friends, and let me tell you What the Lord has done for me;
2. He has written out my par - don In a covenant signed with blood;
3. It is sweet to tell the sto - ry Of his kindness, day by day;
4. Hear the "new song" of re - joic - ing He has taught my heart to sing;

For he saw my bit - ter bond - age, And his mer - cy set me free.
And the Spir - it, dwelling in me, Sheds abroad the "peace of God."
How the flowers of love bloom 'round me, And his smile illumes the way.
Oh, the beau - ty of my Sav - iour! Oh, the glo - ry of my King!

CHORUS.

We will sing it out in heaven, And more sweetness shall be given To the

chords of that eternal harmo- ny;　While the list'ning angels wonder To our

e - ter - nal har - mo - ny;

songs, like mighty thunder, Telling what the Lord hath done for you and me.

Copyright, 1889, by Jno. R. Sweney.

In the Morning.

Lizzie Edwards.

Jno. R. Sweney.

1. We are pilgrims looking home, Sad and wea-ry oft we roam, But we
2. O these tender broken ties, How they dim our aching eyes, But like
3. When our fettered souls are free, Far beyond the narrow sea, And we
4. Thro' our pilgrim journey here, Tho' the night is sometimes drear, Let us

know'twill all be well in the morning; When, our anchor firmly cast, Ev'ry
jewels they will shine in the morning; When our victor palms we bear, And our
hear the Saviour's voice in the morning; When our golden sheaves we bring To the
watch and persevere till the morning; Then our highest tribute raise For the

Fine.

storm-y wave is past, And we gather safe at last   in the morn-ing.
robes immor-tal wear, We shall know each other there, in the morn-ing.
feet of Christ our King, What a chorus we shall sing   in the morn-ing.
love that crowns our days, And to Jesus give the praise   in the morn-ing.

D. S.—sun-ny region bright, When we hail the blessed light of the morn-ing.

CHORUS.

When we all   meet a-gain   in the morn-ing,   On the sweet blooming

D. S.

hills   in the morn-ing; Nev-ermore   to say good night In that

Copyright, 1884, by John J. Hood.

Edward E. Nickerson, by per.

1. Rest to the wea - ry soul And ach - ing breast is given,
2. For thee, my soul, for thee These price - less joys were bought,
3. Come, with the ransomed train, The Sa - viour's prais - es sing,
4. And soon, be-fore his face, We'll praise in light a - bove,

Down where the liv - ing wa - ters flow; Grace makes the wounded whole,
Down where the liv - ing wa - ters flow; Thine is the mer - cy free,
Down where the liv - ing wa - ters flow; Re - joice! the Lamb was slain,
Down where the liv - ing wa - ters flow; Tri - umphant through his grace,

Love fills our heart with heaven, Down where the liv-ing waters flow.
That Christ to earth has brought, Down where the liv-ing waters flow.
A - dore! he reigns a King, Down where the liv-ing waters flow.
Made per - fect by his love, Down where the liv-ing waters flow.

CHORUS.

Down where the living waters flow, Down where the tree of life doth grow, I'm

liv-ing in the light, for Je-sus and the right, Down where the living waters flow

The New Song.

Flora L. Best. Jno. R. Sweney.

Moderato.

1. There are songs of joy that I loved to sing, When my heart was as blithe as a
2. There are strains of home that are dear as life, And I list to them oft 'mid the

bird . . in spring ; But the song I have learned is so full of cheer, That the
din . . of strife; But I know of a home that is wondrous fair, And I

CHORUS. *Vivace.*

dawn shines out in the darkness drear. O, the new, new song! O, the
sing the psalm they are singing there. O, the new, new song!

new, new song, I can sing it now With the
O, the new, new song, I can sing just now With the

ran - som'd throng: . . Pow-er and do - min-ion to him that shall
ransom'd, the ransom'd throng: . .

reign; Glo - ry and praise to the Lamb that was slain.
that shall reign;

3 Can my lips be mute, or my heart be sad, | 4 I shall catch the gleam of its jasper wall
When the gracious Master hath made me | When I come to the gloom of the evenfall,
glad? [be, | For I know that the shadows, dreary and
When he points where the many mansions | dim,
And sweetly says, 'There is one for thee'? | Have a path of light that will lead to him.

From "Gems of Praise," by per.

Fill Me Now.

Rev. E. H. Stokes, D.D.   Jno. R. Sweney.

1. Hov- er o'er me, Ho - ly Spir - it; Bathe my trembling heart and brow;
2. Thou can'st fill me, gracious Spir - it, Tho' I can - not tell thee how;
3. I am weakness, full of weakness; At thy sa - cred feet I bow;
4. Cleanse and comfort; bless and save me; Bathe, oh, bathe my heart and brow!

Fine.

Fill me with thy hal - low'd presence, Come, oh, come and fill me now.
But I need thee, great- ly need thee, Come, oh, come and fill me now.
Blest, di- vine, e - ter - nal Spir - it, Fill with power, and fill me now.
Thou art comfort - ing and sav- ing, Thou art sweet - ly fill - ing now.

D.S. Fill me with thy hal-low'd presence,—Come, oh, come and fill me now.

CHORUS.   D.S.

Fill me now, fill me now, Ho - ly Spir - it, fill me now;

COPYRIGHT, 1879, by JOHN J. HOOD.

Not My Own.

"Ye are not your own, for ye are bought with a price."
1 Cor. vi. 19, 20.

Fr. Nathan.   James McGranahan. By per.

1. "Not my own," but saved by Je - sus, Who redeemed me by his blood,
2. "Not my own!" to Christ, my Saviour, I be - liev - ing, trust my soul;
3. "Not my own!" my time, my tal - ent, Free - ly all to Christ I bring,
4. "Not my own!" the Lord accepts me, One among the ransomed throng,

Glad - ly I ac - cept the mes - sage, I belong to Christ the Lord.
Ev - 'rything to him commit - ted, While e - ter - nal a - ges roll.
To be used in joy - ful ser - vice For the glo - ry of my King.
Who in heaven shall see his glo - ry, And to Je - sus Christ belong.

CHORUS.

"Not my own!" oh, "not my own!" Je - sus, I . . . belong to
oh, no! oh, no! Je - sus, I be - long, be-

thee! All I have, and all I hope for, Thine for all e - ter - ni - ty.
long to thee!

Copyright, 1878, by James McGranahan.

Give Your Heart to Jesus.

Henrietta E. Blair.　　　　　　　　　　　　　Wm. J. Kirkpatrick.

1. Are you wea - ry, sin - oppressed? Give your heart to Je - sus;
2. Would you find sal - va - tion free? Give your heart to Je - sus;
3. Would you know redeem - ing love? Give your heart to Je - sus;

From your bur - den would you rest? Give your heart to Je - sus.
His for - ev - er you may be, Give your heart to Je - sus.
Would you find the joys a - bove? Give your heart to Je - sus.

Are you will - ing now to go Where the cleansing wa - ters flow?
Would you now a bless - ing share? Cast on him your weight of care;
Now his pre - cious word believe; Now his of - fered grace receive;

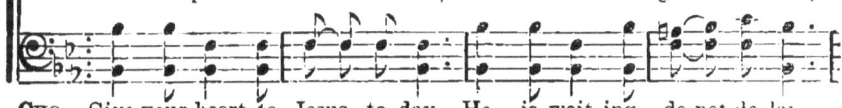

Cho.—Give your heart to Jesus to - day, He is wait - ing,—do not de - lay,—

Repeat for Chorus

You may there be white as snow, Give your heart to Je - sus.
Seek him now by faith and prayer, Give your heart to Je - sus.
Wherefore still the Spir - it grieve? Give your heart to Je - sus.

Seek sal - va - tion while you may, Give your heart to Je - sus.

Copyright, 1885, by Wm. J. Kirkpatrick.

If Any Man Thirst.

J. J. L.

J. J. Lowe.

DUET—Soprano and Tenor.

1. If any man thirst, the Saviour said, The water of life is free;
2. Look unto me and be ye saved, He pleadeth with loving voice;
3. I am the Door; by me, he said, If an-y man en-ter in,
4. I am the Way, the Truth, the Life, Oh, hear our dear Saviour say;

Come unto me and drink and live; O brother, it flows for thee.
Will you not look to Je-sus now, And make him your on-ly choice?
He shall be saved forev-er-more, And fully redeemed from sin.
He bids thee come with all thy sin, Oh, come and be saved to-day.

CHORUS.

Will you not come to him to-day? Will you not come to-day?

Come unto him and drink and live; Oh, will you not come to-day?

Copyright, 1889, by Jno. R. Sweney and Wm. J. Kirkpatrick.

Ye Must be Born Again.

23

"**Verily,** verily, I say unto thee, except a man be born again, he cannot see the kingdom of
W. T. SLEEPER.   God."—John iii. 3.   GEO. C. STEBBINS. By per.

1. A rul - er once came to Jesus by night, To ask him the
2. Ye children of men, at - tend to the word So sol - emn - ly
3. O ye who would enter that glo - ri - ous rest, And sing with the
4. A dear one in heaven thy heart yearns to see, At the beauti - ful

way to salvation and light; The Master made answer in words true and plain, "Ye
uttered by Jesus the Lord, And let not this message to you be in vain, "Ye
ransomed the song of the blest; The life everlasting if ye would obtain, "Ye
gate may be watching for thee; Then list to the note of this solemn refrain, "Ye

CHORUS.

must be born again."   Ye must be born again,   Ye must be born again,

again.   again.   again.

I ver - i - ly, ver - i - ly, say unto thee, Ye must be born again, again.

Eternity.

" Remember how short my time is."—Ps lxxxix. 47.

Mrs. Ellen M. H. Gates.   P. P. Bliss.

1 Oh, the clanging bells of Time! Night and day they never cease; We are
2 Oh, the clanging bells of Time! How their changes rise and fall, But in
3 Oh, the clanging bells of Time! To their voic- es, loud and low, In   a
4 Oh, the clanging bells of Time! Soon their notes will all be dumb, And in

wea- ried with their chime, For they do not bring us peace; And we
un - der - tone sub- lime, Sounding clear - ly through them all, Is   a
long, un - rest - ing line We are marching   to and fro; And we
joy and peace sub- lime, We shall feel the   si - lence come; And our

hush our breath to hear, And we strain our eyes to   see   If thy
voice that must be heard, As our mo- ments on- ward flee, And it
yearn for sight or sound Of the life that is to be, For thy
souls their thirst will slake, And our eyes the King will see, When thy

rit.   *rall.*

shores are draw- ing near,— E - ter - ni - ty! E - ter - ni - ty!
speak- eth aye one word,— E - ter - ni - ty! E - ter - ni - ty!
breath doth wrap us round,— E - ter - ni - ty! E - ter - ni - ty!
glo- rious morn shall break,— E - ter - ni - ty! E - ter - ni - ty!

Used by permission of The J. Church Co., owners of copyright.

Rev. John Love, Jr.   J. J. Lowe.

1. Jesus calls thee, wand'rer, come; Calls to-day, calls to-day; Longs to bid thee welcome
2. Patiently he waits for thee, Waits to-day, waits to-day, Offers full sal- vation
3. He will cleanse your sins away, All away, all away; Why delay the glorious
4. Now he pleads with tender voice, Pleads to-day, pleads to-day, Make his love your
[sacred

home, Home to-day, home to-day; Wondrous love his heart doth feel, Wondrous
free, Free to-day, free to-day; Wouldst thou know his saving grace? Wouldst thou
day? Why de-lay? why de-lay? Oh, the joy you might receive If on
choice, Choose to-day, choose to-day; Shall his pleading be refused? Shall his

S: *Fine.*

love he would reveal, For his own thy life would seal, Seal to-day, seal to-day.
feel his strong embrace, Thro' thy life his favor trace? Yield to-day, yield to-day.
him you would believe, Thought nor fancy can conceive: Don't delay, don't delay.
mer-cy be abused? Come, by grace divine enthused, Come to-day, come to-day.

D.S.—I will cleanse thy sins away; Why delay? why delay?

REFRAIN.   *D.S.*

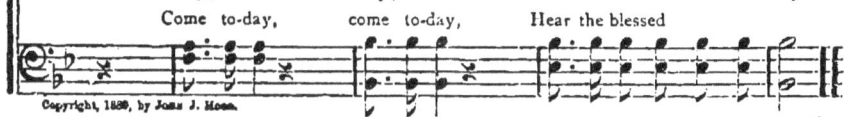

Come to-day, come to-day, Hear the bless - - ed Saviour say:
Come to-day, come to-day, Hear the blessed

Copyright, 1880, by John J. Moss.

How Long?

Julia H. Johnston.

P. Bilhorn. By per

1. To-day the Redeem-er is call-ing, He of-fers his pardon and love,
2. The world and its pleasures are pleading, The tempter is making his claim,
3. Why linger in Satan's dominions? Your doubt and your waiting are vain,

He's "a-ble to keep you from falling, Presenting you faultless" a-bove.
But Je-sus is now in-ter-ced-ing, And longing to call you by name.
Fear not to meet scorn and deri-sion, The Saviour will keep and sustain.

CHORUS.

How long will you keep Jesus waiting? To-day he commands you to choose;

He of-fers a perfect sal-va-tion, And you must accept or re-fuse.

4 How soon will you make the decision?
Oh, what will you gain by delay?
While halting between two opinions,
Your life is fast passing away.

5 'Tis Jesus the Lord and Redeemer
Who asks you this moment to choose;
Be earnest, O trifler and dreamer!
A kingdom and crown you may lose.

Copyright, 1890, by P. Bilhorn.

Nearer the Cross.

"The cross of our Lord Jesus Christ."
Gal. vi. 14.

F. J. CROS

Mrs. J. F. KNAPP. By per.

1. "Near-er the cross!" my heart can say, I am coming near-er, Near-er the
2. Near-er the Christian's mercy seat, I am coming near-er, Feasting my
3. Near-er in prayer my hope aspires, I am coming near-er, Deep-er the

cross from day to day, I am com-ing near-er; Near-er the cross where
soul on man-na sweet, I am com-ing near-er; Stronger in faith, more
love my soul desires, I am com-ing near-er; Near-er the end of

Je-sus died, Near-er the fountain's crimson tide, Near-er my Saviour's
clear I see Je-sus who gave himself for me; Near-er to him I
toil and care, Near-er the joy I long to share, Near-er the crown I

wound-ed side, I am com-ing near-er, I am com-ing near-er.
still would be, Still I'm com-ing near-er, Still I'm com-ing near-er.
soon shall wear: I am com-ing near-er, I am com-ing near-er.

Grace is Free.

Emma M. Johnston.   Wm. J. Kirkpatrick.

1. There's nothing like the old, old sto - ry, Grace is free, grace is free!
2. There's on - ly hope in trusting Je - sus, Grace is free, grace is free!
3. From age to age the theme is tell- ing, Grace is free, grace is free!

Cho.—There's nothing like, etc.

Fine.

Which saints and martyrs tell in glo - ry, Grace is free, grace is free!
From sin that doomed he died to free us, Grace is free, grace is free!
From shore to shore the strains are swelling, Grace is free, grace is free!

It brought them thro' the flood and flame, By it they fought and overcame,
Who would not tell the sto - ry sweet Of love so wondrous, so complete,
And when that time shall cease to be, And faith is crowned with victo - ry,

Use first four lines as Chorus. D. C.

And now they cry thro' his dear name, Grace is free, grace is free!
And fall in rap - ture at his feet, Grace is free, grace is free!
'Twill sound thro' all e - ter - ni - ty, Grace is free, grace is free!

Copyright, 1888, by Wm. J. Kirkpatrick.

The Saviour Precious.

JAMES S. APPLE. JNO. R. SWENEY.

1. { I have found the Saviour precious, And I love him more and more;
     I have found the Saviour precious, And I find him precious still;

2. { I have found the Saviour precious, And, wherev - er I may go,
     I am read - y, if he calls me, In the bat - tle front to stand;

1st.

He has rolled a - way my bur - den, And my mourning days are o'er;
All my life is con - se - crat - ed To his . . . . . .
I will bear the roy - al standard, And its col - ors I will show;
I am read - y—yes, and waiting—To ful - - - - - -

2d **CHORUS.**

service and his will. I have ta - - - ken up the cross, And will
fil my Lord's command. I have taken up the cross, And will nev-er lay it down, I have

nev - - er lay it down Till I see . . . . his face in
taken up the cross, And will nev-er lay it down Till I see his face in glo - ry, Till I

glo - - - ry, And re - ceive . . . . a star - ry crown
see his face in glo - ry, And re - ceive a star - ry crown, a star - ry crown.

3 I have found the Saviour precious;
Hallelujah! praise his name!
To a mansion in his kingdom
Through his grace the right I claim.

I have found the Saviour precious;
He has proved my dearest Friend,
And my faith can trust his promise
Of protection to the end.

Copyright, 1888, by Jno. R. Sweney.

Meet me There.

Henrietta E. Blair.　　　　　　　　　　　　　　Wm. J. Kirkpatrick.

1. On the happy, golden shore, Where the faithful part no more, When the
2. Here our fondest hopes are vain, Dearest links are rent in twain; But in
3. Where the harps of angels ring, And the blest for-ev - er sing, In the

storms of life are o'er, Meet me there; Where the night dissolves away Into
heav'n no throb of pain, Meet me there; By the river sparkling bright, In the
palace of the King, Meet me there; Where in sweet communion blend Heart with

pure and perfect day, I am going home to stay, Meet me there.
ci - ty of delight, Where our faith is lost in sight, Meet me there.
heart, and friend with friend, In a world that ne'er shall end, Meet me there.

Fine.

D.S.—happy golden shore, Where the faithful part no more, Meet me there.

CHORUS.

Meet me there, Meet me there, Where the tree of life is

D.S.

blooming, Meet me there; When the storms of life are o'er, On the

Meet me there;

Copyright, 1885, by Wm. J. Kirkpatrick.

1. Cast thy bread up-on the wa-ters,   Ye   who have but scant supply,
2. Cast thy bread up-on the wa-ters,   Poor and weary, worn with care,—
3. Cast thy bread up-on the wa-ters,   Ye   who have a-bundant store;
4. Cast thy bread up-on the wa-ters,   Far and wide your treasures strew,
5. Cast thy bread up-on the wa-ters,   Waft   it on with praying breath,

An - gel eyes will watch above it;—   You shall find it by   and by!
Oft - en sitting in the shadow,   Have you not a crumb to spare?
It may float on man-y-a bil-low,   It may strand on many-a shore;
Scat - ter it with willing fin-gers,   Shout for joy to see   it   go!
In some distant, doubtful moment   It may save a soul from death;

He   who in his righteous balance   Doth each human ac-tion weigh
Can you not to those around you   Sing some lit-tle song of hope,
You may think it lost for-ev - er,   But,   as sure as God is true,
For   if you do close-ly keep it,   It   will on-ly drag you down;
When you sleep in solemn silence,   'Neath the morn and evening dew,

Will your sac-ri-fice remem-ber,   Will your loving deeds re-pay.
As   you look with longing vision   Thro' faith's mighty tel - e-scope?
In   this life or in the oth - er,   It will yet return   to you.
If   you love it more than Je-sus,   It will keep you from your crown.
Stranger hands, which you have strengthened, May strew lilies over you.

Copyright, 1882, by John J. Hood

Cast thy Burden on the Lord.

"Casting all your care upon him, for he careth for you."
1 Peter v. 7.

W. J. K.

WM. J. KIRKPATRICK.

1. Wea-ry pil-grim on life's pathway, Struggling on beneath thy load,
2. Are thy tir - ed feet unstead - y? Does thy lamp no light af - ford?
3. Are the ties of friendship severed? Hushed the voices fond-ly heard?

Hear these words of con-so - la-tion,—"Cast thy bur - den on the Lord."
Is thy cross too great and hea - vy? Cast thy bur - den on the Lord.
Breaks thy heart with weight of anguish, Cast thy bur - den on the Lord.

CHORUS.

Cast thy bur-den on the Lord, Cast thy bur-den on the Lord, And he will

ad lib.

strengthen thee, sustain and comfort thee ; Cast thy bur - den on the Lord.

4 Does thy heart with faintness falter ?
Does thy mind forget his word?
Does thy strength succumb to weak-
Cast thy burden on the Lord. [ness?

5 He will hold thee up from falling,
He will guide thy steps aright ;
He will strengthen each endeavor;
He will keep thee by his **might**.

Copyright, 1886, by John J. Hood.

" **Let** your light so shine before men, that they may see your good works, and glorify your Father which is in heaven."—Matt. v. 16.

Mrs. E. M. H. Gates.   C. C. Williams.

1.   Say, is your lamp burning, my brother? I pray you look quickly and see ;
2. Upon the dark mountains they stumble, They are bruised on the rocks as they lie
3.   If once all the lamps that are lighted Should steadily blaze in a   line,

For if it were burning, then surely, Some beam would fall brightly on me.
With white, pleading faces turned upward, To the clouds and the pitiful sky.
Wide   o - ver the land and the o - cean, What a girdle of glory would shine !

There are many and many around you,   Who follow wherever you go,
There is   many a lamp that is lighted—We behold them a-near and a-far ;
How all the dark places would brighten! How the mists would turn up and away !

D. S. Say, is your lamp burning, my brother ? I pray you look quickly and see ;

D.S. for Chorus.

If you tho't that they walked in the shadow, Your lamp would burn brighter, I know
But not many among them, my brother, Shine steadily   on like a   star.
How the earth would laugh out in her gladness, To hail the millennial   day !

For if it were burning, then surely, Some beam would fall brightly on me !

Redemption Songs-C   Copyright, 1880, by James McGranahan.

Help Just a Little.

Music from "The Wells of Salvation,"
new words by Rev. W. A. SPENCER.

WM. J. KIRKPATRICK.

1. Brother for Christ's kingdom sighing, Help a lit-tle, help a lit-tle;
2. Is thy cup made sad by tri-al? Help a lit-tle, help a lit-tle;
3. Though no wealth to thee is giv-en, Help a lit-tle, help a lit-tle;

Help to save the mil-lions dy-ing, Help just a lit-tle.
Sweet-en it with self-de-ni-al, Help just a lit-tle.
Sac-ri-fice is gold in heav-en, Help just a lit-tle.

CHORUS.

Oh, the wrongs that we may righten! Oh, the hearts that we may lighten!

Oh, the skies that we may brighten! Helping just a lit-tle.

4 Let us live for one another,
Help a little, help a little;
Help to lift each fallen brother,
Help just a little.

5 Tho' thy life is pressed with sorrow,
Help a little, help a little;
Bravely look t'ward God's to-morrow,
Help just a little.

Copyright, 1885, by JOHN J. HOOD.

Where is Thy Soul?

MARTHA J. LANKTON.   ARTHUR J. SMITH.

1. Oft hast thou heard a voice that said, In tones that were soft and low, Thy
2. Oft hast thou heard a warning voice, That urged thee to fly from sin, To
3. Oft hast thou heard a tender voice, When troubled and care-oppressed, And
4. Oft hast thou heard a grieved, sad voice, Entreating thee o'er and o'er; And

Saviour has loved and loves thee yet, Then why wilt thou slight him so?
open the door you long have closed, And welcome the Saviour   in.
then, like a wea - ry child, hast sighed In Jesus to find   a   rest.
if thou refuse   to hear it now, Perhaps   it will come no more.

CHORUS.

Where is thy soul? where is thy soul? Where is thy soul to-night? That
4th v. Yield to him now, yield to him now, Give him thy soul to-night; That

voice pleads on, pleads patiently on, Oh, where is thy soul to - night?
voice pleads on, pleads patiently on, Oh, give him thy soul to - night?

Copyright, 1868, by Wm J. Kirkpatrick.

Save Me Now.

F. J. C. [From "The Wells of Salvation," by per.] W J. K.

1. Lord, my wayward heart is brok - en, May I come to thee?
2. Tho' I long have grieved thy Spirit, Long re - fused thy grace,
3. Could my faith but touch thy garment Healed my soul would be;
4. Save me now, or I must per - ish, Save me, I im - plore;

In thy gen - tle arms of mer - cy Hast thou room for me?
Do not cast me from thy pres - ence, Do not hide thy face.
Let thy smile of sweet for - give - ness Shed one beam for me.
Speak those lov - ing words so ten - der, "Go and sin no more."

CHORUS.

Save me! save me! Weep-ing at the cross I bow;

Hear my hum-ble sup-pli - ca - tion. Je - sus, save me now.

Copyright, 1881, by John J. Hood.

'Tis the Blessed Hour of Prayer.

"—— went into the temple at the hour of prayer."
Acts iii. 1.

FANNY J. CROSBY.   W. H. DOANE.

1. 'Tis the bless- ed hour of prayer, when our hearts lowly bend, And we
2. 'Tis the bless- ed hour of prayer, when the Saviour draws near, With a
3. 'Tis the bless- ed hour of prayer, when the tempted and tried To the
4. At the bless- ed hour of prayer, trusting him we be - lieve That the

gath - er   to   Je - sus, our Saviour and Friend; If we come to him in
ten - der com - pas- sion his children to hear; When he tells us we may
Saviour who loves them their sorrow con- fide; With a sympathiz - ing
blessing we're needing we'll sure - ly re- ceive, In the fulness of this

faith, his pro-tec - tion to share, What a balm for the wea - ry! O how
cast   at his feet ev - 'ry care, What a balm for the wea - ry! O how
heart he removes ev - 'ry care; What a balm for the wea - ry! O how
trust we shall lose ev - 'ry care; What a balm for the wea - ry! O how

Fine. CHORUS.   D. S.

sweet to   be there! Blessed hour   of prayer, Blessed hour   of prayer;

Copyright, 1880, by Biglow & Main, from " Pure Gold," by per.

Hiding in Thee.

"My strong rock, for a house of defence."
Psa. xxxi. 2.

Rev. William O. Cushing.   Ira D. Sankey. By per.

1. O safe to the Rock that is high - er than I, My soul in the
2. In the calm of the noon-tide, in sorrow's lone hour, In times when temp-
3. How oft in the conflict, when pressed by the foe, I have fled to my

con - flicts and sor- rows would fly; So sin - ful, so wea - ry, thine,
ta - tion casts o'er me its power; In the tem-pests of life, on its
Ref - uge and breathed out my woe; How oft - en, when tri - als like

thine would I be; Thou blest "Rock of A - ges," I'm hid-ing in thee.
wide, heaving sea, Thou blest "Rock of A - ges," I'm hid-ing in thee.
sea - billows roll, Have I hid-den in thee, O thou Rock of my soul.

REFRAIN.

Hiding in thee, Hiding in thee, Thou blest "Rock of Ages," I'm hiding in thee.

He will Gather the Wheat.

HARRIET B. M'KEEVER.   JNO. R. SWENEY.

1. When Je- sus shall gather the na - tions Be- fore him at last to ap- pear,
2. Shall we hear, from the lips of the Saviour, The words, ' Faithful servant, well done;'
3. He will smile when he looks on his children, And sees on the ransomed his seal;

Then how shall we stand in the judgment, When summoned our sentence to hear?
Or, trembling with fear and with anguish, Be banished away from his throne.
He will clothe them in heavenly beau - ty, As low at his footstool they kneel.

CHORUS.

He will gather the wheat in his gar - ner, But the chaff will he scatter a-way;

Then how shall we stand in the judgment, Oh, how shall it be in that day?

4 Then let us be watching and waiting,—
Our lamps burning steady and bright,—
When the Bridegroom shall call to the wed-
Our spirits made ready for flight. [ding]

5 Thus living with hearts fixed on Jesus,
In patience we wait for the time,
When, the days of our pilgrimage ended,
We'll bask in his presence divine

Leaning on Jesus.

Rev. W. F. Crafts.   Wm. J. Kirkpatrick.

1. Wea-ry with walking a - lone, Long heav-y - laden with sin;
2. Fearing to stand for my Lord, Trembling for weakness in prayer;

Toil-ing all night with-out Christ,—Rest for my soul shall I win,
Yet on the bo - som di - vine Los - ing each sor-row and fear,

CHORUS.

Lean - ing on Je - sus, I walk - at his side; . .
Leaning on Je-sus, in him I a - bide. Leaning on Je - sus, I walk at his side;

Lean - - ing on Je - - - sus, I trust him, my Shepherd and Guide.
Leaning on Je-sus, what-ev- er be - tide,

3 Anxious no longer for self.
   Shrinking no longer from pain;
   Leaning on Jesus alone.
   He all my care will sustain.
   Leaning on Jesus, etc.

4 Leaning, I walk in "The Way,"
   Leaning, "The Truth" I shall know;
   Leaning on heart-throbs of Christ,
   Safe into " Life " I may go.
   Leaning on Jesus, etc.

From " Leaflet Gems, No. 2," by per.

Is my Name Written There?

M. A. K.

FRANK M. DAVIS. By per.

1. Lord, I care not for rich - es, Neither sil - ver nor gold; I would make sure of
2. Lord, my sins they are ma-ny, Like the sands of the sea, But thy blood, Oh, my
3. Oh! that beau-ti - ful cit - y, With its mansions of light, With its glo - ri - fied

heaven, I would en - ter the fold. In the book of thy kingdom, With its
Sa-viour! Is suf - fi-cient for me; For thy promise is written, In bright
be - ings, In pure garments of white; Where no e- vil thing cometh, To de -

pa - ges so fair, Tell me, Je - sus, my Sav-iour, Is my name written there?
let - ters that glow, "Though your sins be as scarlet, I will make them like snow."
spoil what is fair; Where the angels are watching, — Is my name written there?

CHORUS.

Is my name writ - ten there, On the page white and fair?

In the book of thy king - dom, Is my name writ - ten there?

God so Loved the World.

FANNY J. CROSBY.   John iii. 16.   WM. J. KIRKPATRICK.

42

Solo ad lib.

1. God loved the world so tenderly His only Son he gave, That all who on his
2. Oh, love that only God can feel, And only he can show! Its height and depth, its
3. Why perish, then, ye ransom'd ones? Why slight the gracious call? Why turn from him
4. O Saviour, melt these hearts of ours, And teach us to believe That whosoever [whose

CHORUS.

name believe Its wondrous pow'r will save. For God so loved the world that he
length and breadth Nor heav'n nor earth can know!
words proclaim E-ter-nal life to all?
comes to thee Shall endless life receive.

gave his on-ly Son, That who-so-ev-er be-lieveth in him

Should not per-ish, should not per-ish; That who-so-ev-er be-

lieveth in him Should not per-ish, but have ev-er-last-ing life.

Copyright, 1886, by Jno. J. Hood.

DO RE MI FA SO LA SI

Jesus, Lover of My Soul.

CHARLES WESLEY.
INO. R. SWENEY.

SOLO.

1. Je - sus, lov - er of my soul! Let me to thy bo - som fly,
2. Oth - er ref - uge have I none; Hangs my helpless soul on thee:
3. Plenteous grace with thee is found, Grace to cov - er all my sin:

While the near - er wa - ters roll, While the tem - pest still is high!
Leave, oh, leave me not a - lone, Still support and com - fort me:
Let the healing streams abound; Make and keep me pure with - in.

CHORUS.

Hide me, O my Saviour, hide, Till the storm of life is past;
All my trust on thee is stayed, All my help from thee I bring;
Thou of life the fountain art, Free-ly let me take of thee:

Safe in - to the hav - en guide, Oh, re - ceive my soul at last!
Cov - er my defenceless head With the sha - dow of thy wing!
Spring thou up within my heart, Rise to all e - ter - ni - ty.

From "Anthems and Voluntaries," by per.

The Waiting Guest.

Mrs. R. N. Turner.   Wm. J. Kirkpatrick.

1. Who is this that waiteth, Waiteth for my call, While the dews of morning
2. Who is this that waiteth In the storm outside, Sad and worn and weary,
3. O, it is my Saviour! Saw I not be - fore All that bleeding sorrow,
4. Thou shalt wait no longer In the gloom outside! Enter, O sweet Stranger,

Gently round him fall? Hark! I hear him knocking, Knocking at my door,
Still his wish de - nied? O, such gentle patience Must an entrance win;
All that anguish sore? Saw I not the nail-prints, When his blood was shed?
And with me a - bide! Long I sought thee, Saviour, Thou wast at my door!

CHORUS.

Asking me for entrance,—Pleading o'er and o'er!
Still I hear him pleading, "Let me enter   in."   Let me in, let me in,
Saw I not the thorn-crown On his king - ly head?
Now I bid thee welcome, Welcome ev - er - more!   O come in, O come in,

Patiently I wait? Wilt thou not unbar the door Ere it be too late?
Be my guest to-day; Saviour, come, abide with me Ev - ermore, I pray.

Copyright, 1894, by John J. Hood.

Have You the Garment of White? 45

" Friend, how camest thou in hither, not having on a
wedding-garment?"—Matt. xxii. 12.

HARRIET JONES.   D. B. TOWNER. By per.

1. The King bids you come and par-take of the feast; For all there is
2. Oh, will you be speechless when questioned by One Who of-fered you
3. Dear friend, are you read - y to meet the great King, And join in 'the

room, ev - en un - to the least; But, if you would en - ter the
mer - cy thro' Je - sus his Son? Who o - pened a fount-ain that
an - them the glo - ri - fied sing? Oh, will you be wel-come with-

pal - ace so fair, The pure wedding garment you sure - ly must wear.
sin - ners be-low Might wear a bright garment as spot-less as snow?
in that pure home, Where none but the white-robed are suffered to come?

CHORUS.

Oh, have you the garment of white, brother, If called to the banquet to-night—

The beautiful garment of white, brother, They wear in the palace of light?

Free Grace.

"Without money and without price."—Isa. lv. 1.

Abbie C. McKeever.

D. B. Towner. By per.

1. Her-ald the tidings to ev - 'ry soul, Wave on wave let the ech - o roll;
2. Sing of the wonderful grace, free grace, Given to all of our ruined race;
3. Go, tell the sto-ry, so grandly true, Praise the Lamb who was slain for you;

Strong and gladly the cho - rus swell, The sto - ry grand of free grace tell.
Shout the sto - ry a - far and near, That ev - 'ry burdened soul may hear.
Shout a - loud of the free grace given, That you and I may dwell in heaven

CHORUS.

Free grace, free grace! Ech - o the cry to a ru - ined race;

Free grace, free grace! Shout, shout the sto - ry of grace, free grace.

Wondrous Love.

J. J. L.

J. J. LOWE.

1. Be - hold, God's won- drous love, Wondrous love, wondrous love,
2. He of - fers you and me Wondrous love, wondrous love!
3. Oh, now this gift re - ceive! Wondrous love, wondrous love!
4. Sweet peace he brings to - day, Wondrous love, wondrous love!

Sent Je - sus from a - bove; Wondrous love, won - drous love!
A par - don full and free; Wondrous love, won - drous love!
And in his name be - lieve; Wondrous love, won - drous love!
Ac - cept it while you may; Wondrous love, won - drous love!

CHORUS.

Oh, this is wondrous love! That Je - sus from a - bove

won - drous love!

His life should give that we might live: Oh, wondrous, wondrous love!

Copyright, 1889, by Jno. R. Sweney and Wm. J. Kirkpatrick.

My Jesus, I Love Thee.

" Mine are thine and thine are mine."

" London Hymn Book."

John xvii. 10.

A. J. GORDON. By per.

1. My Je - sus, I love thee, I know thou art mine,
2. I love thee be - cause thou have first lov - ed me,
3. I will love thee in life, I'll love thee in death,
4. In man - sions of glo - ry and end - less delight,

For thee all the fol - lies of sin I re - sign;
And pur - chased my par - don on Cal - va - ry's tree;
And praise thee as long as thou lend - est me breath;
I'll ev - er a - dore thee in heav - en so bright;

My gra - cious Re - deem - er, my Sav - iour art thou,
I love thee for wear - ing the thorns on thy brow;
And say, when the death - dew lies cold on my brow,
I'll sing with the glit - ter - ing crown on my brow,

If ev - er I loved thee, my Je - sus, 'tis now.

J. J. Lowe.

1. I heard the voice of Je - sus say, "Come un - to me and rest; Lay
2. I heard the voice of Je - sus say, "Be-hold, I free - ly give The
3. I heard the voice of Je - sus say, " I am this dark world's light; Look

down, thou wea - ry one, lay down Thy head up - on my breast." I
liv - ing wa - ter, thirst - y one, Stoop down, and drink, and live." I
un - to me, thy morn shall rise, And all thy day be bright." I

came to Je - sus as I was—Wea - ry, and worn, and sad; I
came to Je - sus, and I drank Of that life - giv - ing stream; My
looked to Je - sus, and I found In him my Star, my Sun; And

found in him a rest - ing-place, And he has made me glad.
thirst was quenched, my soul revived, And now I live in him.
in that Light of Life I'll walk Till trav -'ling days are done.

Copyright, 1868, by John J. Hood. *Redemption Songs—D*

Tell it to Jesus.

J. E. Rankin, D.D.   Matt. xiv. 12.   E. S. Lorenz. By per.

1. Are you wea-ry, are you heavy-hearted? Tell it to Je-sus,
2. Do the tears flow down your cheeks un-bidden? Tell it to Je-sus,
3. Do you fear the gath'ring clouds of sorrow? Tell it to Je-sus,
4. Are you troubled at the thought of dying? Tell it to Je-sus.

Tell it to Je-sus; Are you grieving o-ver joys de-part-ed?
Tell it to Je-sus; Have you sins that to man's eye are bidden?
Tell it to Je-sus; Are you anxious what shall be to-mor-row?
Tell it to Je-sus; For Christ's coming Kingdom are you sigh-ing?

CHORUS.

Tell it to Je-sus a-lone. Tell it to Je-sus, tell it to Je-sus,

He is a friend that's well known; You have no oth-er

such a friend or broth-er, Tell it to Je-sus a-lone.

Tell Me the Story of Jesus.

FANNY J. CROSBY.　　　　　　　　　　　　　JNO. R. SWENEY.

1. Tell me the sto - ry of Je - sus, Write on my heart ev -'ry word,
2. Fasting, a- lone in the des - ert, Tell of the days that he passed,
3. Tell of the cross where they nailed him, Writhing in anguish and pain;

CHO.—Tell me the sto - ry of Je - sus, Write on my heart ev'ry word,

Fine.

Tell me the sto - ry most precious, Sweetest that ev - er was heard;
How for our sins he was tempted, Yet was triumphant at last;
Tell of the grave where they laid him, Tell how he liv - eth a- gain;

Tell me the sto - ry most precious, Sweetest that ev - er was heard.

Tell how the angels, in cho - rus, Sang as they welcomed his birth -
Tell of the years of his la - bor, Tell of the sorrow he bore,
Love in that sto - ry so ten - der, Clear - er than ev - er I see;

D. C.

Glo - ry to God in the high - est! Peace and good tidings to earth.
He was despised and af- flict - ed, Homeless, reject - ed and poor.
Stay, let me weep while you wisper, Love paid the ransom for me.

Copyright, 1880, by John J. Hood.

52 That's the News.

Arr. by J. R. S.

Jno R. Sweney.

1. Whene'er we meet you always say, What's the news? What's the news?
2. The Lamb was slain on Calva - ry; That's the news! That's the news!
3. The Lamb has pardoned all my sin; That's the news! That's the news!
4. He took my sorrows all a way; That's the news! That's the news!

Pray, what's the order of the day? What's the news? What's the news?
To set a world of sin-ners free; That's the news! That's the news!
I feel the witness deep with-in; That's the news! That's the news!
He turned my darkness in-to day; That's the news! That's the news!

Oh, I have glorious news to tell,—My Saviour hath done all things well, And
'Twas there his precious blood was shed,'Twas there he bowed his sacred head, But
And since he took my sins away, And taught me how to watch and pray, I'm
Yes, Jesus saves me now, I know, His blood has washed me white as snow, And

triumphed over death and hell; That's the news! That's the news!
now he's ris - en from the dead; That's the news! That's the news!
hap - py now from day to day; That's the news! That's the news!
now I'm glad his love to show,—That's the news! That's the news!

5 His work's reviving all around;
　　That's the news!
And many have redemption found;
　　That's the news! [flame,
And since their souls have caught the
They shout hosanna to his name,
And all around they spread his fame;
　　That's the news!

6 O weary pilgrim, hear the call,
　　Blessed news!
Christ Jesus came to save us all;
　　That's the news!
He died to set poor sinners free,
That we from death might ransomed be,
And with him reign eternally;
　　That's the news!

Copyright, 1800, by Jno R Sweney

The Master is Calling.

Rev. E. H. Stokes, D. D.   Jno. R. Sweney.

1. The Master is calling for you, dear friend, The Master is calling for
2. He calls by his Word unto you, dear friend, His Word which has come from a-
3. He calls by his Spir-it to you, dear friend, His Spirit is moving your

you; You have wandered away,—Won't you come back to-day? Come
bove, Won't you heed it to-day? Won't you come to him, say? Come
heart; Won't you yield to him now? Won't you here make your vow, For

CHORUS.

back to the good and the true. Come, the dear Master is call - ing,
back to the heart of his love.
heaven at once you will start.

Come, the dear Master is call - ing, Call - ing, call - ing, Is
Calling for you,   calling for you,

tender - ly calling for you.
for you.

4 He calls by his providence, too, dear
     friend,
In ways which have sorrows untold;
Though your spirit may sigh,
Let your fond heart reply,
Dear Lord, I'll return to thy fold.

5 The Master is calling you all, dear
The Master is calling us, too; [friends,
We have wandered away,
Let us come back to-day,
Come back to the good and the true.

Copyright, 1888, by Jno. R. Sweney.

The Saviour is My All in All.

P. P.   *"Wherefore he is able to save them to the uttermost."*—Heb. vii. 25.   P. Bilhorn.

1. The Saviour is my all in all, He is my constant theme!
2. His Spir- it gives sweet peace within, And bids all care de - part!
3. And whatso- ev - er I may ask, To glo - ri - fy his name,
4. Oh, praise the Lord, my soul, rejoice, Give thanks unto thy God!

rit.

By sim - ply trusting in his word He keeps me pure and clean.
He fills my soul with righteousness, And pu - ri - fies the heart.
The Fa - ther free - ly gives to me, Since Christ the Saviour came.
Who took thee in thy sin - fulness, And cleansed thee by his blood!

CHORUS.

Glo - ry! oh, glo - ry! Je - sus hath redeemed me;

rit.

Glo - ry! oh, glo - ry! He washed my sins a - way. a - way!

Copyright, 1880, by P. Bilhorn.

Only a Step.

55

FANNY J. CROSBY.

"'Then come thou, for there is peace.'"
1 Sam. xx. 21.

W. H. DOANE. By per.

1. On-ly a step to Jesus! Then why not take it now? Come, and, thy sin con-
2. On-ly a step to Jesus! Believe, and thou shalt live; Lovingly now he's
3. On-ly a step to Je-sus! A step from sin to grace; What hast thy heart de-
4. On-ly a step to Je-sus! O why not come, and say, Gladly to thee, my

REFRAIN.

fess - ing, To him thy Saviour bow.   On-ly a step, On-ly a step;
wait- ing, And read-y to for - give.
cid - ed? The moments fly a - pace.
Sav-iour, I give myself a - way.

Come, he waits for thee; Come, and, thy sin confessing, Thou shalt receive a

bless-ing; Do not re-ject the mer-cy He free-ly of-fers thee.

Copyright, 1873, by Biglow & Main, from "Royal Diadem," by per.

Coming To-Day.

Fanny J. Crosby.   Jno. R. Sweney.

1. Out on the des-ert, looking, looking, Sinner, 'tis Je-sus looking for thee;
2. Still he is waiting, waiting, waiting, O, what compassion beams in his eye,
3. Lovingly pleading, pleading, pleading, Mercy, tho' slighted, bears with thee yet;
4. Spirits in glory, watching, watching, Long to behold thee safe in the fold;

Tender - ly calling, calling, calling, Hither, thou lost one, O, come unto me.
Hear him repeat-ing gent-ly, gently, Come to thy Saviour, O, why wilt thou die.
Thou canst be happy, hap-py, hap-py, Come, ere thy life-star forever shall set.
Angels are waiting, waiting, waiting, When shall thy story with rapture be told?

CHORUS.

Jesus is looking, Jesus is calling, Why dost thou linger, why tarry away?

Run to him quickly, say to him gladly, Lord, I am coming, coming to-day.

Copyright, 1880, by John J. Hood.

Trusting Jesus, That is All.

"Though he slay me, yet will I trust him."
Job xiii. 15.

Rev. Edgar Page Stites.　　　　　　　　　　　　Ira D. Sankey. By per

1. Sim - ply trusting ev - 'ry day, Trust-ing thro' a storm - y way;
2. Bright-ly doth his Spir - it shine In - to this poor heart of mine:
3. Sing - ing, if my way is clear; Pray-ing, if the path is drear:
4. Trust-ing him while life shall last, Trust-ing him till earth is past:

Ev - en when my faith is small, Trusting Je - sus, that is all.
While he leads I can - not fall, Trusting Je - sus, that is all.
If in dan - ger, for him call; Trusting Je - sus, that is all.
Till with-in the jas - per wall, Trusting Je - sus, that is all.

CHORUS.

Trust - ing as the mo - ments fly, Trust-ing as the days go by;

Trust - ing him, whate'er be-fall, Trust-ing Je - sus, that is all.

Give me Jesus.

Fanny J. Crosby.

Jno R. Sweney.

1. Take the world, but give me Je - sus,—All its joys are but a name;
2. Take the world, but give me Je - sus, Sweetest com - fort of my soul;
3. Take the world, but give me Je - sus, Let me view his constant smile;
4. Take the world, but give me Je - sus, In his cross my trust shall be,

But his love a - bid - eth ev - er, Thro' e - ter - nal years the same.
With my Sav - iour watching o'er me I can sing, though billows roll.
Then throughout my pilgrim jour - ney Light will cheer me all the while.
Till, with clear - er, brighter vis - ion, Face to face my Lord I see.

CHORUS.

Oh, the height and depth of mer - cy! Oh, the length and breadth of love!

Oh, the ful - ness of redemption, Pledge of end - less life a - bove!

Copyright, 1889, by Jno. R. Sweney.

When the King comes in.

J. E. LANDOR.   Rev. E. S. LORENZ.

1. Called to the feast by the King are we, Sit-ting, perhaps, where his
2. Crowns on the head where the thorns have been, Glo - ri -fied he who once
3. Like lightning's flash will that instant show Things hidden long from both
4. Joy - ful his eye shall on each one rest Who is in white wedding

peo - ple be: How will it fare, then, with thee and   me,
died for men; Splen - did the vis - ion be - fore us   then,
friend and foe, Just what we are ev' - ry one will know,
gar - ments dressed—Ah! well for us if we stand the test,

REFRAIN.

When the King comes in? When the King comes in, brother, When the King comes

in! How will it fare with thee and me When the King comes in ?

He Has Come.

Mrs. J. H. Knowles. Zech. ix. 9. Mrs. J. F. Knapp. By per.

1. He has come! he has come! my Redeem- er has come, He has tak - en my
2. He has come! he has come! my Love and my Lord, Ev'ry thought of my
3. He has come! he has come! O hap - pi- est heart, He has giv - en his
4. He has come to abide, and ho - ly must be The place where my

heart as his own chosen home; At last I have given the welcome he sought.
being is swayed by his word; He-has come, and he rules in the realm of my soul,
word that he will not depart; No trou- ble can en - ter, no e - vil can come
Lord deigns to banquet with me; And this is my pray'r, Lord, since thou art come,

CHORUS.

He has come, and his coming all gladness has brought. Joy! joy is mine, my
And his scep-tre is love, O bless - ed control!
To the heart where the God of peace has his home.
Make meet for thy presence my heart as thy home.

Sav- iour divine Comes to abide with me, with me, with me, Comes to abide,

rit.

ev - er to a- bide. My own lov- ing Saviour a - bid - eth with me.

When Jesus Comes.

P. P. B.

"Unto them that look for him shall he appear the second time, without sin, unto salvation.—Heb. ix, 28.

P. P. BLISS.

1. Down life's dark vale we wander, Till Jesus comes; We watch and wait and
2. Oh, let my lamp be burning When Jesus comes ; For him my soul be
3. No more heart-pangs nor sadness, When Jesus comes; All peace and joy and
4. All doubts and fears will vanish, When Jesus comes; All gloom his face will

CHORUS.

wonder, Till Je-sus comes. All joy his loved ones bringing,
yearning, When Jesus comes.
gladness, When Jesus comes.
ban-ish, When Jesus comes.

When Jesus comes;

All praise thro' heaven ringing, When Jesus comes; All beauty bright and vernal

When Je-sus comes; All glo-ry, grand, e-ter-nal, When Je-sus comes

5 He'll know the way was dreary,
　　When Jesus comes;
He'll know the feet grew weary,
　　When Jesus comes.

6 He'll know what griefs oppressed me,
　　When Jesus comes;
Oh, how his arms will rest me!
　　When Jesus comes.

By permission of The J. Church Co., owners of copyright.

Wait, and Murmur Not.

W. H. BELLAMY.   WM. J. KIRKPATRICK.

1. The home where changes never come, Nor pain nor sorrow, toil nor care ; Yes!
2. Yet when bow'd down beneath the load By heav'n allow'd, thine earthly lot Thou
3. If in thy path some thorns are found, O, think who bore them on his brow ; If
4. Toil on, nor deem, tho' sore it be, One sigh unheard, one prayer forgot; The

'tis   a bright and blessed home ; Who would not fain be resting there ?
yearnst to reach that blest a - bode, Wait, meekly wait, and murmur not.
grief   thy sorrowing heart has found, It reached a ho - li - er than thou.
day   of rest will dawn for thee ; Wait, meekly wait, and murmur not.

CHORUS.

O,   wait, meek - ly wait, meek - ly wait, and mur - mur not,   O,

wait, meek-ly wait, meekly wait, and murmur not,   O,   wait, meek-ly wait,

O,   wait, meekly wait, O, wait, and mur - mur not. O, murmur not.

By permission of John J. Hood, owner of copyright.

Jesus will Save You now.

HENRIETTA E. BLAIR. WM. J. KIRKPATRICK.

1. Come, oh, come to the ark of rest,— Je - sus will save you now;
2. Come, oh, come to the ark of grace,— Je - sus will save you now;
3. Come, oh, come to the ark of love,— Je - sus will save you now;
4. Who'll be first to a - rise for prayer? Je - sus will save you now;

Come, with the weight of your guilt oppressed, Je - sus will save you now.
Haste to his arms and his dear embrace, Je - sus will save you now.
Come, like the worn and wea - ry dove, Je - sus will save you now.
Who'll be the first the cross to bear? Je - sus will save you now.

CHORUS.

Come while your cheeks with tears are wet, Come ere the star of life shall set,

Come, and the step you will ne'er re - gret, Je - sus will save you now.

Copyright, 1882, by John J. Hood.

God be with You.

" The grace of our Lord Jesus Christ be with you."
Rom. xvi. 20.

J. E. RANKIN, D. D.   W. G. TOMER.

1. God be with you till we meet again, By his counsels guide, uphold you,
2. God be with you till we meet again,'Neath his wings securely hide you;
3. God be with you till we meet again,When life's perils thick confound you;
4. God be with you till we meet again, Keep love's banner floating o'er you;

With his sheep securely fold you, God be with you till we meet again.
Dai - ly manna still provide you, God be with you till we meet again.
Put his arms unfailing round you, God be with you till we meet again.
Smite death's threat'ning wave before you,God be with you till we meet again.

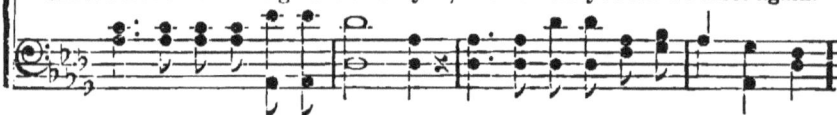

CHORUS.

Till we meet, till we meet, Till we meet at Je - sus' feet;
Till we meet, till we meet, till we meet, till we meet;

Till we meet, till we meet, God be with you till we meet again.
Till we meet, till we meet, till we meet,

From " Gospel Bells," by per.

Watching for the Bridegroom.

JAMES NICHOLSON.　　　　　　　　　　　　　　　　　JNO. R. SWENEY.

1. Our Je - sus says that he will come. To gath - er home his own,
2. That this may be our hap- py lot, Let us be on our guard,
3. The fool - ish ones, with lamps gone out, Too late their oil would buy,

And at the sup- per of the Lamb We shall with him sit down.
Or else he'll say, "I know you not," When once the door is barred.
For, lo, at midnight comes the shout, Behold! the Bridegroom's nigh.

CHORUS.

Then we'll watch . . . for the Bridegroom, Watch, watch, watch,

Then we'll watch for the Bridegroom, Watch while our lamps we trim;

Then we'll watch for the Bridegroom, And with him enter in.

Then we'll watch for the Bridegroom,

4 Oh, when we hear the Bridegroom's
　At morning or at night, 　　　[cry,
　May all our hopes on Christ rely,
　And all our lamps be bright.

5 And when we join the blood-washed
　And sing the song divine, 　[throng,
　This strain shall burst from every tongue,
　The glory, Lord, be thine.

Redemption Songs—E　　Copyright in "Goodly Pearls," by John J. Hood.

Gathering Home.

Miss Mariana B. Slade.

R. N. M'Intosh. By per.

1. Up to the bounti-ful Giv-er of life,—Gathering home! gathering home!
2. Up to the city where falleth no night,—Gathering home! gathering home!
3. Up to the beautiful mansions above,—Gathering home! gathering home!

Up to the dwelling where cometh no strife, The dear ones are gathering home.
Up where the Saviour's own face is the light, The dear ones are gathering home.
Safe in the arms of his in-finite love, The dear ones are gathering home.

CHORUS.

Gath-er-ing home! . . . . . gath-er-ing home! . . . . .
Gath-er-ing home!
gath-er-ing home!

Nev-er to sorrow more, never to roam; Gathering home! . . . . .
Gath-er-ing home!

gath-er-ing home! . . . . God's children are gather-ing home.
gath-er-ing home!

A Smile from Jesus.

FANNY J. CROSBY. [From "The Wells of Salvation," by per.] JNO. R. SWENEY.

1. Tho' kin-dred ties around us Like i - vy branches twine, Tho'
2. We meet in Christian con - verse, We speak of joys to come, We
3. One look, one smile from Je - sus, For whom our souls would live, Not

life has man - y pleas-ures That o'er my path-way shine, Tho'
lift our eyes ex-pect - ant To E - den's bliss- ful home; Tho'
heav'n's transcendant beau - ty Such ho - ly joy can give; Be-

words to friend-ship sa - cred More sweet than mu - sic fall, One
sweet and prec - ious bless-ings With ev - 'ry mo - ment fall, One
yond the si - lent riv - er Though spir - it voic - es call, One

Fine.

D. S. look, one smile from Je - sus Is dear - er far than all.

CHORUS. D. S.

Dear - er, yes, dear - er, Dear - er far than all, One
Dearer than all, dear-er than all, Dear-er, yes, dear - er far than all.

Copyright, 1881, by JOHN J. HOOD.

Go Work.

Rev. John Love, Jr.

J. J. Lowe.

1. In the Mas - ter's vine - yard, There is work to do;
2. Sweet the joy of ser - vice, Let none i - dle prove;
3. Fee - ble gifts the Sav - iour Gra - cious - ly will use;
4. Haste ye, ere the dark - ness Swift - ly gath - ers o'er,

While the hours are fleet - ing, Christ hath need of you.
Faith - ful toil for Je - sus Best re - veals our love.
Can the loy - al ser - vant His be - hest re - fuse?
And the day of la - bor Dawn for thee no more.

CHORUS.

Stand no long - er i - dle, Work be - gin to - day;

Christ for you is call - ing, call - ing, Cheerful - ly o - bey.

Copyright, 1889, by Jno. R. Sweney and Wm. J. Kirkpatrick.

Entire Consecration.

FRANCES RIDLEY HAVERGAL.   Chorus by W. J. K.   WM. J. KIRKPATRICK.

1. Take my life, and let it be   Con - se - crat - ed, Lord, to thee;
2. Take my feet, and let them be   Swift and beau - ti - ful for thee;
3. Take my lips, and let them be   Filled with mes - sag - es for thee;
4. Take my moments and my days,   Let them flow in endless praise;

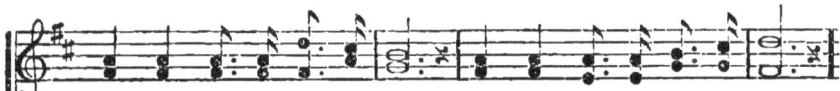

Take my hands and let them move   At the impulse of thy love.
Take my voice and let me sing   Al - ways, on - ly, for my King.
Take my sil - ver and my gold,—   Not a mite would I withhold.
Take my in - tel - lect, and use   Ev - 'ry power as thou shalt choose.

CHORUS.

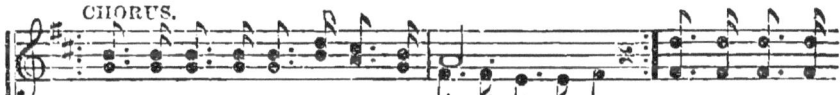

{ Wash me in the Saviour's precious blood, the precious blood, } Lord, I give to
{ Cleanse me in its pu - ri - fy - ing flood, the healing flood, }

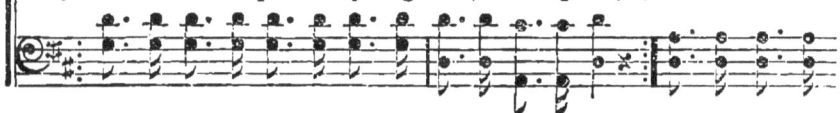

thee, my life and all, to be, Thine, henceforth, e - ter - nal - ly.

5 Take my will, and make it thine;
  It shall be no longer mine;
  Take my heart,—it is thine own,—
  It shall be thy royal throne.

6 Take my love,—my Lord, I pour
  At thy feet its treasure-store!
  Take myself, and I will be
  Ever, only, all for thee!

70 Casting Your Care Upon Him.

JAMES L. BLACK.   JNO. R. SWENEY.

1. Child of God, be not discouraged, Cast thy bur - den on the Lord;
2. O'er the dark and troubled waters, Tho' you oft may stem the tide,
3. Child of God, no power can harm you, Naught of ill your soul molest,
4. Soon your eyes with joy will see him, Soon your feet will press the shore,

With a cheer - ful, lov - ing spir - it Read and trust his gracious word.
Not a - lone you brave the temptest,—He is there your Friend and Guide.
Casting all your care on Je - sus, In his arms you safe - ly rest.
Where the saints redeemed are waiting, And the storms of life are o'er.

CHORUS.

Cast-ing all . . . . . your care upon him, ... When your
Cast - ing all your care upon him, Cast - ing all your care upon him, When your

skies . . . with clouds are dim, . . . You will find . . . the promise
skies with clouds are dim, When your skies with clouds are dim, You will find the promise

true, ... Je - sus careth, Je - sus car-eth still for you. . . . .
true, the promise true,   careth for you.

Copyright, 1900, by Jno. R. Sweney.

Bringing in the Sheaves.

"The harvest is the end of the world."—Matt. xiii. 39.

Words from "Songs of Glory." GEO. A. MINOR. By per.

1. Sowing in the morning, sowing seeds of kindness, Sowing in the noon-tide,
2. Sowing in the sunshine, sowing in the shadows, Fearing neither clouds nor
3. Go, then, ev- er weeping, sowing for the Master, Though the loss sustained our

and the dew- y eves; Waiting for the har- vest, and the time of reap - ing,
winter's chilling breeze; By and by the harvest, and the la - bor end - ed,
spir-it oft - en grieves; When our weeping's over, he will bid us wel-come,

CHORUS.

We shall come rejoicing, bringing in the sheaves. Bringing in the sheaves,
bringing in the sheaves,

1.
We shall come rejoic- { ing,. bringing in the sheaves, }
{ Omit second time, . . . }

2.
-ing, bringing in the sheaves.

Tell it Again.

Mrs. M. B. C. Slade.   R. M. McIntosh.

1. In - to the tent where a gyp- sy boy lay, Dy- ing a - lone at the
2. "Did he so love me,—a poor lit - tle boy? Send unto me the good
3. Bending we caught the last words of his breath, Just as he entered the
4. Smiling, he said, as his last sigh he spent, "I am so glad that for

close of the day, News of sal - va - tion we car- ried, said he,
tid - ings of joy? Need I not per - ish? my hand will he hold?
val - ley of death;"God sent his Son!"—"whoso - ev - er?" said he;
me he was sent!" Whispered, while low sank the sun in the west,

REFRAIN.

"No - bo - dy ev - er has told it to me!" Tell it a - gain!
No - bo - dy ev - er the sto - ry has told!"
"Then I am sure that he sent him for me!"
"Lord, I be- lieve, tell it now to the rest!"

Tell it a- gain! Sal- vation's sto- ry repeat o'er and o'er, Till none can

say of the children of men, "No- bo - dy ev - er has told me be- fore."

By permission.

Welcome Bells of Heaven.

PRISCILLA J. OWENS. WM. J. KIRKPATRICK.

Moderato.

1. Hear the welcome bells of heav-en Call-ing weary wand'rers home,—
2. Come, ye sad and heav-y-lad-en, With the weight of sin oppressed,
3. Leave your doubts and fears behind you, Whoso-ev-er will may come;
4. Poor way-far-er, old and lone-ly, Come, 'tis dark and growing late,

Come where peace and joy are giv-en, Come to Je-sus,—all may come.
At his feet cast down your burden, Christ will give you sweetest rest.
Leave the darkness and the dang-er, Christ will guide you safely home.
En-ter now the door of mer-cy, Kindest welcomes for you wait.

CHORUS.

Come to Je-sus, come to Je-sus,— Hark! the
Hear the bells of heav-en ring-ing, hear the bells of heav-en ring-ing, Call-ing wea-ry

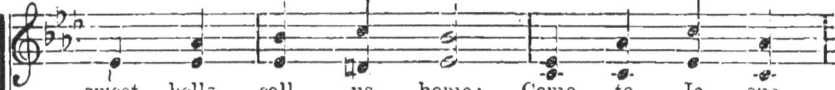

sweet bells call us home; Come to Je-sus,
wand'rers, call-ing wea-ry wand'rers home; Come where peace and joy are given,

Repeat pp

come to Je-sus, Come and wel-come.— all may come.
come where peace and joy are given, Come and welcome, come and welcome,—all may come.

5 Little children, too, are welcome:
  "Suffer them to come to me;"
  Blessed Saviour, thou art calling;
  Help us all to come to thee.

6 When in mansions bright we gather
  In the Palace of the King,
  "Come, ye blessed of my Father,"
  Sweetly shall the joy bells ring.

Copyright, 1888, by WM. J. KIRKPATRICK.

It Reaches Me.

MARY D. JAMES.　　　　　　　　　　　　　　　　　　JNO. R. SWENEY.

1. Oh, this ut - ter-most sal - va - tion! 'Tis a fountain full and free,
2. How a - maz - ing God's compassion, That so vile a worm should prove
3. Je - sus, Saviour, I a - dore thee! Now thy love I will proclaim,

Pure, ex-haustless, ev - er flow - ing, Wondrous grace! it reaches me!
This stupend - ous bliss of Heav-en, This un-measured wealth of love!
I will tell the blessed sto - ry, I will mag - ni - fy thy name!

CHORUS.

It reaches me! it reaches me! Wondrous grace! it reaches me!

Pure, ex-haustless, ev - er flowing, Wondrous grace! it reaches me!

From "The Garner," by per.

DO RE MI FA SO LA SI

The Stranger at the Door.

Rev. iii. 20.

T. C. O'KANE.

75

1. Behold   a stranger at the door, He gently knocks—has knocked before
2. O love - ly at - titude,—he stands With melting heart and open hands;
3. But will he prove a friend indeed? He will,—the very friend you need;

Has wait-ed long, is wait-ing still; You treat no oth - er friend so ill.
O matchless kindness, and he shows This matchless kindness to his foes.
The friend of sin - ners? Yes, 'tis he, With garments dyed on Cal- va - ry.

CHORUS.

Oh, let the dear Saviour come in,   He'll cleanse the heart from sin; Oh,
             come in,   from sin;

keep him no more out at the door, But let the dear Saviour come in. come in.

4 Rise, touched with gratitude divine,
Turn out his enemy and thine;
That soul-destroying monster, Sin,
And let the heavenly Stranger in.

5 Admit him, ere his anger burn,—
His feet, departed, ne'er return;
Admit him, or the hour's at hand
You'll at his door rejected stand.

By permission.

Are You Washed in the Blood?

E. A. H.

Rev. E. A Hoffman. By per.

1. Have you been to Jesus for the cleansing power? Are you washed in the
2. Are you walking dai - ly by the Saviour's side? Are you washed in the
3. When the Bridegroom cometh will your robes be white, Pure and white in the
4. Lay a- side the garments that are stained with sin, And be washed in the

blood of the Lamb? Are you ful- ly trusting in his grace this hour? Are you
blood of the Lamb? Do you rest each moment in the Cru - ci- fied? Are you
blood of the Lamb? Will your soul be ready for the mansions bright, And be
blood of the Lamb? There's a fountain flowing for the soul unclean, O be

CHORUS.

washed in the blood of the Lamb? Are you washed in the
Are you washed

blood, In the soul-cleansing blood of the Lamb? Are your
in the blood, of the Lamb?

garments spotless? are they white as snow? Are you washed in the blood of the Lamb?

James L. Black.   Jno. R. Sweney.

1. God is here, and that to bless us With the Spirit's quick'ning power;
2. God is here! we feel his presence In this con - se- crat- ed place;
3. God is here! oh, then, believ - ing, Bring to him our one de- sire,
4. Saviour, grant the prayer we of- fer, While in sim - ple faith we bow,

See, the cloud alread - y bend- ing, Waits to drop the grateful shower.
But we need the soul- re- fresh- ing Of his free, unbounded grace.
That his love may now be kindled, Till its flame each heart inspire.
From the windows of thy mer - cy Pour us out a blessing now.

CHORUS.

Let it come,   O Lord, we pray thee, Let the shower of blessing fall;
Let it come,   Let the shower

We are wait - ing, we are waiting, Oh, revive the hearts of all.
We are waiting,   Oh, re- vive

Copyright, 1880, by Jno. R. Sweney.

78 Where Mother Knelt in Prayer.

Thos. MacKellar.   J. J. Lown.

1. Once in my boyhood's gladsome day, My spirits light as air,   I
2. Her hands were clasped in ferven - cy, Her lips gave forth no sound, Yet,
3. My moth - er, all entranced in prayer, My presence heeded not, And
4. An orphaned wand'rer, far from home, In af - ter time I strayed; But

wan- dered to   a lone - ly room Where mother knelt in prayer, Where
awe-struck, solemn - ly   I felt   I stood on ho - ly ground—Where
rev - 'rent- ly   I turned a - way In si - lence from the spot—Where
God has kept me, and   I feel He heard her when she prayed, He

moth - er knelt in   prayer, Where moth-er knelt in prayer, I
moth - er knelt in   prayer, Where moth-er knelt in prayer, I
moth - er knelt in   prayer, Where moth-er knelt in prayer, I
heard her when she prayed, He heard her when she prayed. But

wan - dered to   a lone - ly room Where moth-er knelt in prayer.
felt   I stood on ho - ly ground, Where mother knelt in prayer.
turned in si - lence from the spot Where moth-er knelt in prayer.
God has kept me, and   I feel He heard her when she prayed.

Copyright, 1879, by Jno. R. Sweney and Wm. J. Kirkpatrick.

Labor On.

C. R. BLACKALL. W. H. DOANE. By per.

Spirited.

1. In the har- vest field there is work to do, For the grain is ripe and the
2. Crowd the garner well with the sheaves all bright, Let the song be glad and the
3. In the gleaner's path may be rich reward, Tho' the time seems long and the
4. Lo! the harvest home in the realms above Shall be gained by each who has

reap - ers few, And the Mas-ter's voice bids the work-ers true Heed the
heart be light, Fill the precious hours, ere the shades of night Take the
la - bor hard; For the Mas-ter's joy, with his chosen shared, Drives the
toiled and strove, When the Master's voice, in sweet words of love, Calls a-

Fine. CHORUS.

call that he gives to- day. Labor on, labor on, Keep the
place of the gold-en day.
gloom from the darkest day.
way to e-ter-nal day. la-bor on, la-bor on,

D.S.—on till the close of day.

D. S.

bright reward in view; 'Tis the Saviour's command, He will strength renew, Labor

I Hope to Meet You All in Glory.

EMMA PITT. WM. J. KIRKPATRICK.

1. I hope to meet you all in glo - ry, When the storms of life are o'er;
2. I hope to meet you all in glo - ry, By the tree of life so fair;
3. I hope to meet you all in glo - ry, Round the Saviour's throne above;
4. I hope to meet you all in glo - ry, When my work on earth is o'er;

I hope to tell the dear old sto - ry, On the bles-sed shin-ing shore.
I hope to praise our dear Redeem- er For the grace that brought me there.
I hope to join the ransomed arm - y Singing now redeem-ing love.
I hope to clasp your hands rejoic- ing On the bright e - ter - nal shore.

CHORUS.

On the shin - ing shore, On the gold - en strand, In our

Father's home, In the hap - py land: I hope to meet you there, I

hope to meet you there,—A crown of vict -'ry wear,—In glo - ry.

Copyright, 1884, by John J. Hood.

Sweet Peace, the Gift of God's Love. 81

P. H. ROBLIN.   P. BILHORN.

1. There comes to my heart one sweet strain, A glad and a joyous re - frain,
   sweet strain,   refrain,
2. By Christ on the cross peace was made, My debt by his death was all paid,
   was made,   all paid,
3. When Jesus as Lord I had crowned, My heart with this peace did abound,
   had crowned,   abound.
4. In Jesus for peace I a- bide, abide, And as I keep close to his side, his side,

I sing   it a-gain and a - gain, Sweet peace, the gift of God's love.
No oth - er founda- tion is   laid   For peace, the gift of God's love.
In him the rich blessing I found, Sweet peace, the gift of God's love.
There's nothing but peace doth betide, Sweet peace, the gift of God's love.

CHORUS.

Peace, peace, sweet peace! Won- der- ful gift from a - bove! a-bove! Oh,

won- derful, wonder- ful   peace! Sweet peace, the gift   of God's love!

Redemption Songs - F   Copyright, 1887, by P. Bilhorn.

82 Are You Coming While He Calls?

P. B.   P. BILHORN By per.

1. You have heard the Gospel message, You have heard it o'er and o'er, He that
2. Is there one will now believe him, Is there one who'll turn from sin, Is there
3. Will you give yourself to Jesus, Will you give yourself to God, Will you
4. Are you coming? are you coming? You have wandered far from God, There is

heareth and believeth Shall have life forever more; Oh, then why will you re-
one will now receive him, And the heavenly life begin, Is there one who knows his
trust his love and mercy, Will you trust his precious blood? Will you come unto the
pardon freely offered, There is cleansing in the blood! Are you coming? are you

fuse him, Oh, then why will you delay To believe and trust in Jesus, Who will
weakness, Is there one who knows his need? Will you come while he is calling, Will you
fountain, Which for sin was opened wide, Will you come while he is calling, Come un-
coming, Ere the judgment on you falls? See, the night is fast approaching, Are you

CHORUS.

wash your sins away. Are you com - ing, are you com - ing? There's a
now the Spirit heed?
to the crimson tide?   Are you coming,   are you coming?
coming while he calls?

welcome and a pardon for you all, for you all, Are you com - - ing

Copyright, 1894, by P. Bilhorn.

rit.

while he calls, ... Are you coming while the Sav-iour calls?

are you coming while he calls,

Hide Thou Me.

FANNY J. CROSBY.   *"Thou art my hiding place."*—Ps. xxxii. 7.   ROBERT LOWRY. By per.

1. In thy cleft, O Rock of a-ges, Hide thou me; When the fitful tempest
2. From the snare of sinful pleasure, Hide thou me; Thou, my soul's eternal
3. In the lonely night of sorrow, Hide thou me; Till in glory dawns the

ra-ges, Hide thou me; Where no mortal arm can sev-er From my
trea-sure, Hide thou me; When the world its power is wielding, And my
mor-row, Hide thou me; In the sight of Jordan's bil-low, Let thy

heart thy love forev-er, Hide me, O thou Rock of a-ges, Safe in thee.
heart is almost yielding, Hide me, O thou Rock of a-ges, Safe in thee.
bo-som be my pillow; Hide me, O thou Rock of a-ges, Safe in thee.

Copyright, 1880, by BIGLOW & MAIN.

3

Will Jesus Find us Watching?

FANNY J. CROSBY.   [From "Gospel Music," by per.]   W. H. DOANE.

1. When Je - sus comes to re - ward his servants, Whether it be
2. If at the dawn of the ear - ly morning, He shall call us
3. Have we been true to the trust he left us? Do we seek to
4. Bles - sed are those whom the Lord finds watching, In his glo - ry

noon or night, Faith - ful to him will he find us watching,
one by one, When to the Lord we re - store our tal - ents,
do our best? If in our hearts there is naught condemns us,
they shall share; If he shall come at the dawn or midnight,

rit.   REFRAIN.

With our lamps all trimm'd and bright.   Oh, can we say we are
Will he ans - wer thee—Well done?
We shall have a glo - rious rest.
Will he find us watch - ing there?

rea - dy, brother? Rea - dy for the soul's bright home? Say, will he

find you and me still watching, Waiting, waiting when the Lord shall come?

Copyright, 1870, by W. H. DOANE.

Jesus Saves.

PRISCILLA J. OWENS.   WM. J. KIRKPATRICK.

1. We have heard a joy - ful sound, Je - sus saves, Je - sus saves;
2. Waft it on the roll - ing tide, Je - sus saves, Je - sus saves;
3. Sing a - bove the bat - tle's strife, Je - sus saves, Je - sus saves;
4. Give the winds a might - y voice, Je - sus saves, Je - sus saves;

Spread the glad - ness all a- round, Je - sus saves, Je - sus saves;
Tell to sin - ners, far and wide, Je - sus saves, Je - sus saves;
By his death and end - less life, Je - sus saves, Je - sus saves;
Let the na - tions now re - joice, Je - sus saves, Je - sus saves;

Bear the news to ev' - ry land, Climb the steeps and cross the waves,
Sing, ye is - lands of the sea, E - cho back, ye o - cean caves,
Sing it soft - ly thro' the gloom, When the heart for mer - cy craves,
Shout sal - va - tion full and free, High- est hills and deepest caves,

Onward, 'tis our Lord's command, Je - sus saves, Je - sus saves.
Earth shall keep her ju - bi - lee, Je - sus saves, Je - sus saves.
Sing in tri - umph o'er the tomb, Je - sus saves, Je - sus saves.
This our song of vic - to - ry, Je - sus saves, Je - sus saves.

Copyright, 1882, by John J. Hood.

Fair Portals.

F. A. B.   "He hath prepared for them a city."—Heb. xi. 16.   F. A. BLACKMER.

1. Swing back for one moment, fair portals Of that wondrous city, we pray;
2. One glimpse shall our courage embolden, And brighten the whole of our way;
3. We've read of that city's bright glory, That knows not the darkness of night;
4. We've read of the Tree and the Riv- er, Life's water and fruit ev-er fair;
5. Those gates we're approaching, how cheering! Oh, let us prove faithful alway;

One glimpse, and the fears of these mortals Shall vanish forev - er away.
Oh, why should the sight be withholden? By faith we would view it to-day.
And reading that wonderful sto - ry Has ravished our souls with delight.
We've looked up in faith to the Giver, And prayed that we might enter there.
And know, as the city we're nearing, That they shall to us some sweet day

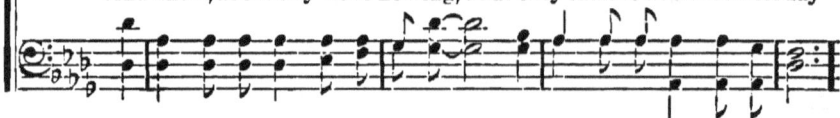

CHORUS.

Swing o - pen,   fair por- tals,   A moment, and let us look thro';
Last v. Swing o - pen,   those por- tals,   And we shall in triumph go in,
Swing o- pen,   fair portals,

One glimpse, and we faltering mor - tals   To enter shall press on a- new.
Where we shall as ransom'd immortals   E- ter - nit- y blessed be- gin.

Copyright, 1891, by John J. Hood.

The Morning Draweth Nigh.

Fanny J. Crosby.

Jno. R. Sweney.

1. Oh, ral - ly round the stand- ard Of Christ, our roy - al King; Oh.
2. Tho' long and deep the sha - dows The dreary night may bring, Our
3. To yon-der gold - en reg - ion Our faith now plumes her wing; Our
4. To him who paid our ran - som, And took from death the sting, Be

CHORUS.

ral - ly round his stand- ard, And hal - le - lu - jahs sing. For the
lamps are trimm'd and burn- ing, Our hal - le - lu - jahs ring.
hearts with joy are bound- ing, And hal - le - lu - jahs ring.
ev - er - last- ing prais - es, Let hal - le - lu - jahs ring.

morn - - - ing draweth nigh, For the morn - - -
morning draweth nigh, For the morning draweth nigh, Hal - le - lu - jah! hal- le-

- - - ing draweth nigh; We can see . . . it in the
lu - jah! yes, the morn- ing draw-eth nigh; We can see it, we can

dis - tance, We shall hear it, we shall hear it by and by. by and by.
see it in the distance,

Copyright, 1889, by Jno. R. Sweney.

Can a Boy Forget his Mother?

J. H. W.　　　　　　　　　　　Rev. J. H. Weber.　By per.

1. Can a boy forget his mother's prayer, When he has wandered, God knows
2. Can a boy forget his mother's face, Whose heart was kind and filled with
3. Can a boy forget his mother's door, From which he wandered years be-
4. Can a boy forget that she is dead, Though many years have passed and

[same!]

where? Its down the path of death and shame, But mother's prayers are heard the
grace? Her loving voice it echoes sweet; She waits, she longs her boy to meet!
fore? With tears and sighs she said, "Good-bye, Meet me, my boy, beyond the sky!"
fled? Those tears, that prayer, that sweet "Good-bye;"

She waits to welcome thee on high:

CHORUS.

Come back, my boy, come back, I say, And walk now in thy mother's

way! Come back, my boy, come back, I say, And walk now in thy mother's way.

Copyright, 1885, by Rev. J. H. Weber.

Glory to Jesus, He Saves.

P. B.

P. BILHORN.

1. Glo - ry to Je - sus who died on the tree, Paid the great price that my
2. Once in my heart there was sin and despair, Now the dear Saviour him-
3. Come, then, ye wea-ry, who long to be free, Come to the Saviour, he

soul might be free; Now I can sing hal - le - lu - jah to God,
self dwelleth there, And from his pres-ence comes peace to my soul,
wait - eth for thee; Then with the ransomed this song you can sing,

CHORUS.

Glo - ry! he saves, he saves. Glo - ry! he saves, glo - ry! he saves,

Saves a poor sin - ner like me; Glo - ry! he saves,

glo - ry! he saves, Saves a poor sin - ner like me. like me.

Copyright, 1885, by P. Bilhorn.

Redeemed.

"Let the redeemed of the Lord say so."
Ps. cvii. 2.

HARRIET JONES.   D. B. TOWNER. By per.

1. Oh, glad "whoso-ev-er," the deed is done, My sins are pardoned thro'
2. I came to my Saviour, his word believed, When he the sin-ner
3. Oh, glad "whoso-ev-er," the crimson tide Is free and o-pen, is

Christ the Son. Of love so precious I never had dreamed, Oh, sweet is the
once received, And now his praises I joy-ful-ly sing, And dwell in the
deep and wide; Oh, come, my brother, and bathe in the stream, And you shall be

CHORUS.

peace of the soul redeemed. Oh, glo - - - ry to Je - - sus, re-
love of my Lord and King.
filled with a joy supreme. Oh, glo-ry to Je-sus, my soul is redeemed! my

deemed!   re - deemed!   Of love so precious I never had dreamed, Oh,
soul is redeemed! my soul is redeemed!

rap - - turous sto - - ry, re - deemed!   re - deemed!   Oh,
rap-turous sto- ry, my soul is redeemed! my soul is redeemed! my soul is redeemed! Oh,

rall.

glo - - - ry! oh, glo - - ry, re - deemed! re - deemed!

glo - ry, oh, glo - ry, my soul is redeemed, my soul is redeemed, my soul is redeemed.

Jesus Loves Me.

P. P. Bliss.　　　　John iv. 19.　　　　D. B. Towner. By per.

1. Je - sus loves me, I'm his child, Though by na- ture sin - de- filed;
2. Je - sus all my grief doth know, Measures well my cup of woe;
3. Je - sus will not send a pain Which to me shall not be gain;
4. Je - sus soon will call me home; There no pain nor grief can come;

Yet he washed me, made me clean, Dwells himself my heart with - in.
Knows, for he the path hath trod, Bore for me the wrath of God.
Nor in an - ger deal the blow; Strength to bear it will be- stow.
Then on Ca- naan's peaceful shore I shall praise him ev - er- more.

CHORUS.

Je - sus loves me, praise his name, I am cleansed from ev - 'ry stain;

I have plunged beneath the flood, I'm redeemed thro' Je - sus' blood.

Why Do You Wait?

G. F. R.　　　　"Arise, he calleth thee." Mark x. 49.　　　　Geo. F. Root.

1. Why do you wait, dear brother,　Oh, why do you tarry so long? Your
2. What do you hope, dear brother,　To gain by a further de - lay? There's
3. Do you not feel, dear brother,　His Spirit now striving within? Oh,
4. Why do you wait, dear brother,　The harvest is passing a - way, Your

Saviour is waiting to give you　A place in his sanc - ti - fied throng.
no one to save you but Je - sus, There's no other way but his way.
why not accept his sal - va - tion, And throw off thy burden of sin?
Saviour is longing to bless you, There's danger and death in delay?

CHORUS.

Why not? why not? Why not come to him now?

Why not? why not? Why not come to him now?

By per. of The John Church Co.　　　　DO RE MI FA SO LA SI

Seeking for Me.

E. E. HASTY.

1. Jesus, my Saviour, to Bethlehem came, Born in a manger to sorrow and shame;
2. Jesus, my Saviour, on Calvary's tree, Paid the great debt, and my soul he set free;
3. Jesus, my Saviour, the same as of old, While I did wander afar from the fold,
4. Jesus, my Saviour, shall come from on high, Sweet is the promise as weary years fly;

Oh, it was wonder-ful, blest be his name, Seeking for me, for me.
Oh, it was wonder-ful, how could it be? Dy-ing for me, for me.
Gent-ly and long he hath pled with my soul, Calling for me, for me.
Oh, I shall see him descending the sky, Coming for me, for me.

for me, ... for me; . . . .

Seeking for me, seeking for me, Seeking for me, seeking for me
Dy-ing for me, dying for me, Dy-ing for me, dying for me;
Call-ing for me, calling for me, Call-ing for me, calling for me
Com-ing for me, coming for me, Com-ing for me, coming for me,

Oh, it was wonderful, blest be his name, Seeking for me, for me.
Oh, it was wonderful, how could it be? Dy-ing for me, for me.
Gent-ly and long he hath pled with my soul, Calling for me, for me.
Oh, I shall see him descending the sky, Coming for me, for me.

By per. of Towne & Stillman.

94 While the Days are Going By.

Geo. Cooper. By per.   Jno. R. Sweney.

1. There are lone-ly hearts to cherish, While the days are going by; There are
2. There's no time for i - dle scorning, While the days are going by; Let our
3. All the lov-ing links that bind us While the days are going by, One by

wear - y souls who per - ish While the days are go - ing by.   If   a
face be like the morning, While the days are go - ing by.   Oh, the
one we leave behind us While the days are go - ing by.   But the

smile we can renew, As our journey we pursue, Oh, the good that we might do,
world is full of sighs, Full of sad and weeping eyes; Help your fallen brother rise
But the seeds of good we sow, Both in shade and shine will grow, And will keep our
                                                              [hearts aglow,

CHORUS.

While the days are going by. While going by,   while going by,
                              while going by,   while going by,

Oh, the good we may be do-ing, While the days are go-ing by.

From "Gems of Praise," by per.

Jesus will Help You.

WM. STEVENSON.   [From "Good as Gold, by per."]   REV. R. LOWRY.

1. The Sav-iour is calling you, sin-ner—Urg-ing you now to draw nigh;
2. Thro' him there is life in be-liev-ing; Sin-ner, O why will you die?
3. There's danger in longer de-lay-ing, Swift-ly the moments pass by;

He asks you by faith to re-ceive him; Je-sus will help if you try.
Ac-cept him by faith as your Saviour; Je-sus will help if you try.
If now you will come, there is mercy; Je-sus will help if you try.

REFRAIN.

Jesus will help you, Jesus will help you, Help you with grace from on high; The

weakest and poorest the Saviour is calling; Jesus will help if you try.

Copyright. 1875, by BIGLOW & MAIN.

Redeemed, Praise the Lord.

Jennie Mills. WM. J. KIRKPATRICK.

1. O happy day! what a Sav-iour is mine! I am redeemed, praise the Lord!
2. O clap your hands, all ye people of God, I am redeemed, praise the Lord!
3. Thanks be to God for the great vict'ry given, I am redeemed, praise the Lord!
4. Glory to God, I would shout ev - ermore, I am redeemed, praise the Lord!

Fine.

All to his pleasure I glad - ly re-sign, I am redeemed, praise the Lord!
Let ev'ry tongue speak his mercy abroad, I am redeemed, praise the Lord!
Now I am free; ev'ry chain has been riven,—I am redeemed, praise the Lord!
O for a voice that could reach ev'ry shore, I am redeemed, praise the Lord!

Key C.

Jesus has taken my burden away; Jesus has turned all my night into day;
His loving-kindness is better than gold; He doth bestow more than my cup can hold
Out of the pit, and the mire, and the clay, Jesus has borne me in triumph away;
Help me, ye ransom'd, awake, ev'ry string, Let earth rejoice and the whole heavens ring,

Use first four lines as Chorus. D. C.

Jesus has come to my heart,—come to stay,—I am redeemed, praise the Lord!
Wondrous Salvation, that ne'er can be told,—I am redeemed, praise the Lord!
Safe on the rock I am standing to - day,—I am redeemed, praise the Lord!
While we the chorus u - ni - ted-ly sing, I am redeemed, praise the Lord!

Copyright, 1886, by John J. Hood.

DO RE MI FA SO LA SI

H. G. SPAFFORD.   " He hath delivered my soul in peace."—Ps. lv. 18.   P. P. BLISS.

1. When peace, like a riv - er, at - tend- eth my way, When sorrows, like
2. Though Satan should buffet, though trials should come, Let this blest as-
3. My sin—oh, the bliss of this glo - rious thought—My sin—not in
4. And, Lord, haste the day when the faith shall be sight, The clouds be rolled

sea - bil-lows, roll; What-ev - er my lot, thou hast taught me to
sur - ance con - trol, That Christ hath re-gard - ed my help-less es-
back as a scroll, The trump shall resound, and the Lord shall depart, but the whole, Is nailed to his cross and I bear it no

CHORUS.

say, It is well, it is well with my soul.   It is well . . . .
tate, And hath shed his own blood for my soul.
more, Praise the Lord, praise the Lord, oh, my soul!   It is
scend, "Ev - en so"—it is well with my soul.

. . . . with my soul, ... It is well, it is well with my soul.
well   with my soul,

By per. of The John Church Co., owners of copyright.   *Redemption Songs*—G

Why Don't You Come?

L. W. Munhall.

C. R. Dundar. By per.

1. O ye wand'rers, come to Je - sus, He is call-ing you to - day;
2. You are need- y, lost, and wea - ry; You are sick and wounded sore;
3. Do not think your works have merit, Cast your deadly goodness down'
4. Do not wait until you're bet - ter, For you sure- ly will be lost;

By his sovereign grace he frees us: Come, be saved while now you may.
Long have trod the way most dreary; Can you ev - er need him more?
Not by these can you in - her - it Life e - ternal—heaven's crown.
Come, he'll break sin's ev'ry fet - ter; Come, at once, at an - y cost.

REFRAIN.

Why don't you come to Je - sus? He's wait- ing to receive you, Why

1st. *2d.*

don't you come to Je - sus and be saved? saved?

5 He from heaven came to save you,
Hung upon th'-accursed tree,
'Rose from death to justify you,
Waits to intercede for thee.

6 Yield just now, in glad submission,
In repentance, faith, and love;
He will grant you full remission,
Take you to his home above.

Lord of All.

EDWARD PERRONET.   J. J. LOWE.

1. All hail the power o.   Je - sus' name! Let an - gels prostrate fall;
2. Ye chos - en seed of Is - rael's race, Ye ransomed from the fall,
3. Sin-ners, whose love can ne'er for-get The wormwood and the gall,
4. Let ev - 'ry kind - red, ev - 'ry tribe, On this ter - res - trial ball,
5. O that with yon - der sa - cred throng We at his feet may fall!

Bring forth the roy - al   di - a - dem, And crown him Lord of all.
Hail him who saves you   by his grace, And crown him Lord of all.
Go, spread your trophies at his feet, And crown him Lord of all.
To him all ma - jes - ty as - cribe, And crown him Lord of all.
We'll join the ev - er - last - ing song, And crown him Lord of all.

REFRAIN.

Crown him, crown him Lord   of all, Crown him, crown him Lord   of all;

crown him Lord of all,   crown him Lord of all;

Bring forth the roy - al   di - a - dem, And crown him Lord of all.

Copyright, 1889, by John J. Hood.

100 Weeping will not Save Me.

"For by grace are ye saved through faith."
Eph. ii. 8.

R. L.　　　　　　　　　　　　　　　　Rev. R. Lowry. By per.

1. Weeping will not save me—Tho' my face were bathed in tears, That could not al-
2. Working will not save me—Purest deeds that I can do, Holiest thoughts and
3. Waiting will not save me—Helpless, guilty, lost, I lie; In my ear is
4. Faith in Christ will save me—Let me trust thy weeping Son, Trust the work that

lay my fears, Could not wash the sins of years—Weeping will not save me.
feelings too, Can not form my soul anew—Working will not save me.
mercy's cry; If I wait I can but die—Waiting will not save me.
he has done; To his arms, Lord, help me run—Faith in Christ will save me.

Fine.

D. S.—Je-sus waits to make me free, He a-lone can save me.

REFRAIN.

Je-sus wept and died for me; Je-sus suffered on the tree;

101 Give Us Light.

L. W. Munhall.　　　　　　　　　　　　Jno. R. Sweney.

1. Give us light for life e-ter-nal; Send us fire the dross to burn;
2. Take our hearts, our wills, our passions, Naught of self would we retain;
3. All in all thou art un-to us, Light and fire, and joys and love;

Copyright, 1889, by Jno. R. Sweney.

Give Us Light.—CONCLUDED.

Fine

Let us know the joys su-per-nal; For thy love our spirits yearn
What we yield are thy pos-ses-sions, And, by yielding, Christ we gain.
Flood and burn, and thrill and fill us, Seal us for the life a-bove.

D.S.—Give us light for life e-ter-nal; Send us fire the dross to burn.

CHORUS. |D.S.

Give . . . us light, . . . Give . . us light. . . .

102

Bright Canaan.

OLD MELODY.

Fine.

1 { Togeth-er let us sweetly live, I am bound for the land of Canaan;
    Togeth-er let us sweetly die, I am bound for the land of Canaan. }

D.S.—hap-py home, I am bound for the land of Canaan.

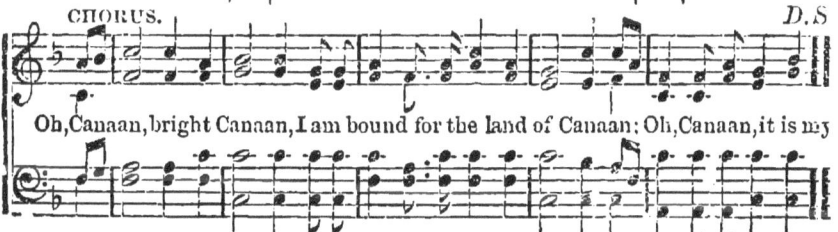

CHORUS. D.S

Oh, Canaan, bright Canaan, I am bound for the land of Canaan; Oh, Canaan, it is my

2 If you get there before I do,
   I am bound for the land of Canaan;
Then praise the Lord, I'm coming too,
   I am bound for the land of Canaan.

3 Part of my friends the prize have won,
   I am bound for the land of Canaan;
And I'm resolved to follow on,
   I am bound for the land of Canaan.

4 Then come with me, beloved friend,
   I am bound for the land of Canaan;
The joys of heaven shall never end,
   I am bound for the land of Canaan.

5 Our songs of praise shall fill the skies,
   I am bound for the land of Canaan;
While higher still our joys shall rise,
   I am bound for the land of Canaan.

Jerusalem the Golden.

Bernard of Cluny.   Tr. by J. M. Neale.   Tune, EWING.   7, 6.

1. Je - rusalem the golden, With milk and honey blest, Beneath thy contem-
pla - tion Sink heart and voice opprest: I know not, oh, I know not What
joys a- wait us there; What radiancy of glory, What light beyond compare.

2 They stand, those halls of Zion,
   All jubilant with song,
And bright with many an angel,
   And all the martyr throng:
The Prince is ever in them,
   The daylight is serene;
The pastures of the blessed
   Are decked in glorious sheen.

3 There is the throne of David;
   And there, from care released,
The song of them that triumph,
   The shout of them that feast;

And they who, with their Leader,
   Have conquered in the fight,
Forever and forever
   Are clad in robes of white.

4 O sweet and blessed country,
   The home of God's elect!
O sweet and blessed country
   That eager hearts expect!
Jesus, in mercy bring us
   To that dear land of rest;
Who art with God the Father,
   And Spirit, ever blest.

104   Love Divine.

Charles Wesley.   Tune, LOVE DIVINE. 8, 7, d.

1. Love di-vine, all love ex - cel- ling, Joy of heaven, to earth come down!

Love Divine.—CONCLUDED.

Fine.

Fix in us thy hum- ble dwelling! All thy faith-ful mer- cies crown.

D.S.—Vis - it us with thy sal - va- tion; En - ter ev - 'ry trembling heart.

D.S.

Je - sus, thou art all com - pas- sion, Pure, unbounded love thou art;

2 Breathe, oh, breathe thy loving Spirit
Into every troubled breast!
Let us all in thee inherit,
Let us find that second rest.
Take away our bent to sinning;
Alpha and Omega be;
End of faith, as its beginning,
Set our hearts at liberty.

3 Come, almighty to deliver,
Let us all thy life receive;
Suddenly return, and never,
Never more thy temples leave;

Thee we would be always blessing,
Serve thee as thy hosts above,
Pray, and praise thee without ceasing,
Glory in thy perfect love.

4 Finish then thy new creation;
Pure and spotless let us be;
Let us see thy great salvation,
Perfectly restored in thee:
Changed from glory into glory,
Till in heaven we take our place,
Till we cast our crowns before thee,
Lost in wonder, love, and praise.

105 Jesus, Meek and Gentle.

GEORGE R. PRYNNE.

Tune, GUIDANCE. 6, 5.

1. Jesus, meek and gen- tle, Son of God Most High, Pitying, loving
2. Pardon our of- fenc - es, Loose our captive chains, Break down ev'ry

Sav - iour, Hear thy children's cry.
i - dol Which our soul de- tains.

3 Give us holy freedom,
Fill our hearts with love;
Draw us, holy Jesus,
To the realms above.

4 Lead us on our journey,
Be thyself the way
Through terrestrial darkness
To celestial day.

5 Jesus, meek and gentle, etc

1. Sav-iour, Hear thy chil - - - - - **103**

On the Way.

Lizzie Edwards.

Jno. R. Sweney.

1. O, bless the Lord, what joy is mine! What perfect peace thro' grace divine!
2. O, bless the Lord, he dwells with me, The voice I hear, the hand I see
3. O, bless the Lord for what I know Of heavenly bliss while here below!
4. O, bless the Lord 'twill not be long Till I shall join the ho-ly throng,

Fine.

And now to realms of end-less day, O, bless the Lord, I'm on the way.
Renew my strength from day to day While home to him I'm on the way.
My trusting heart thro' faith can say, To mansions bright I'm on the way.
And shout and sing thro' endless day, Where every tear is wiped a-way.

D.S.— crown to wear in end-less day, O, bless the Lord, I'm on the way.

CHORUS.

D.S.

I'm on the way, I'm on the way, In vain the world would bid me stay: A

Copyright, 1-90, by Jno. R. Sweney.

107 Follow All the Way.

Geo. W. Collins.

Arr. by Wm. J. Kirkpatrick.

1. I have heard my Saviour calling, I have heard my Saviour calling,
2. Tho' he leads me thro' the valley, Tho' he leads me thro' the valley,
3. Tho' he leads me thro' the garden, Tho' he leads me thro' the garden,

Cho.—Where he leads me I will follow, Where he leads me I will follow,

Copyright, 1894, by Wm. J. Kirkpatrick.

Follow All the Way.—CONCLUDED.

I have heard my Saviour calling, "Take thy cross and follow, follow me."
Tho' he leads me thro' the valley, I'll go with him, with him all the way.
Tho' he leads me thro' the garden, I'll go with him, with him all the way.

Where he leads me I will follow, I'll go with him, with him all the way.

4 ‖: Tho' the path be dark and dreary, :‖
I'll go with him, with him all the way.

5 ‖: Tho' he leads me to the conflict, :‖
I'll go with him, with him all the way.

6 ‖: Tho' he leads through fiery trial, :‖
I'll go with him, with him all the way.

7 ‖: I will follow on to know him :‖
He's my Saviour, Saviour, Brother
Friend.

8 ‖: He will give me grace and glory, :‖
He will keep me, keep me all the way.

9 ‖: O 'tis sweet to follow Jesus, :‖
And be with him, with him all the way.

108 The Blood's Applied.

R. K. C.

R. KELSO CARTER.

Fine.

1. { The blood's applied! my soul is free, I'm saved, without, with- in;
{ The blood of Je - sus cleanseth me From ev - 'ry trace of sin.

D.S.—blood's applied, I'm sanc - ti - fied, It makes me pure with - in.

D.S.

The blood's applied, I'm jus - ti- fied, It par- dons ev- 'ry sin; The

2 I've bid farewell to every fear,
By faith I claim the prize;
Now I can read my title clear
To mansions in the skies.

3 Temptations come and trials too,
While hellish darts are hurled;
But Jesus saves me through and
In spite of all the world. [through,

4 Though cares and storms and sorrows
About me thick and fast, [fall
My Jesus,—he is Lord of all,—
Will bring me home at last.

5 Then will my happy, happy soul
Tell of his love and rest,
While shouts of victory shall roll
From every conquering breast.

Copyright 1896, by John J. Hood.

There'll be Joy by and by.

Mrs. E. C. Ellsworth.   "Joy cometh in the morning."—Ps. xxx. 5.   Rev. R. Lowry. By per.

1. Tho' the night be dark and dreary, Tho' the way be long and wea-ry,
2. Tho' thine eyes are sad with weeping, Thro' the night thy vigils keeping,
3. Tho' thy spir - it faints with fasting Thro' the hours so slowly wasting,

Morn shall bring thee light and cheer; Child, look up, the dawn is near.
God shall wipe thy tears a-way, Turn thy dark-ness in-to day.
Morn shall bring a glo-rious feast, Thou shalt sit an honored guest.

CHORUS.

There'll be joy by and by, There'll be joy by and by,

In the dawning of the morning, There'll be joy by and by.

ril.

110 # Lead Me, Precious Saviour.

Mrs. J. F. K.   Mrs. Jos. F. Knapp. By per.

1. Lead me, lead me, Lead me, precious Saviour, In-to the narrow way, In-
2. I will love thee, Ev-er, ev-er love thee; May sinful thoughts depart, Oh,
3. Lead me, fold me, Guide, and ever keep me, And thanks my heart will give, Dear

CHORUS.

to the narrow way, Fold me, fold me, Fold me to thy bo-som, And
take them from my heart.
Saviour, while I live.

may I never stray, oh, nev-er stray, And I will praise thee ev-ermore, yes,

ev - er - more, And I will praise thee ev-ermore, yes, ev - er - more.

111   Angels Hovering Round.

1. There are angels hov'ring round, There are angels hov'ring round, There are
2. They will carry the tid-ings home, They will carry the tidings home, They will

an - gels, an - gels hov'ring round.
car - ry, car - ry the tid-ings home.

3 To the New Jerusalem,
    etc.

4 Poor sinners are coming
    home, etc.

5 And Jesus bids them
    come, etc.

6 There's glory all around,
    etc.

112 Revive us again.

WM. P. MACKAY.   J. J. HUSBAND.

1. We praise thee, O God! for the Son of thy love,
For Jesus who died and is now gone above.

REFRAIN.

Hal-le-lujah! thine the glory; Halle-lujah! a-men! Revive us a-gain.

2 We praise thee, O God! for thy Spirit of light,
Who has shown us our Saviour and scattered our night.

3 All glory and praise to the Lamb that was slain,
Who has borne all our sins, and has cleansed every stain.

4 All glory and praise to the God of all grace,
Who has bought us, and sought us, and guided our ways.

113 While Jesus Whispers to You.

WILL. F. WITTER.   H. R. PALMER.

1. { While Je-sus whispers to you, Come, sinner, come!
While we are praying for you, Come, ... sin-ner, come!

{ Now is the time to own him, Come, sinner, come!
Now is the time to know him, Come, ... sin-ner, come!

2 Are you too heavy laden?
Come, sinner, come!
Jesus will bear your burden,
Come, sinner, come!
Jesus will not deceive you,
Come, sinner, come!
Jesus can now redeem you,
Come, sinner, come!

3 Oh, hear his tender pleading,
Come, sinner, come!
Come and receive the blessing,
Come, sinner, come!
While Jesus whispers to you,
Come, sinner, come!
While we are praying for you,
Come, sinner, come?

Copyright, 1878, by H. R. Palmer.

Depth of Mercy.

1. Depth of mer - cy! can there be Mer - cy still reserved for me?

Can my God his wrath for - bear,— Me, the chief of sin-ners, spare?

2 I have long withstood his grace;
Long provoked him to his face;
Would not hearken to his calls;
Grieved him by a thousand falls.

3 Now incline me to repent;
Let me now my sins lament;
Now my soul revolt deplore,
Weep, believe, and sin no more.

4 Kindled his relentings are;
Me he now delights to spare;
Cries, "How shall I give thee up?"
Lets the lifted thunder drop.

5 There for me the Saviour stands,
Show his wounds and spreads his
God is love! I know, I feel; [hands;
Jesus weeps, and loves me still.

I Do Believe.

1. A - las! and did my Sav - iour bleed? And did my Sovereign die?
Cho.— I do be - lieve, I now be - lieve, That Je - sus died for me:

Would he de - vote that sacred head For such a worm as I?
And thro' his blood, his precious blood, I shall from sin be free.

2 Was it for crimes that I have done
He groaned upon the tree?
Amazing pity! grace unknown!
And love beyond degree.

3 Well might the sun in darkness hide,
And shut his glories in,
When God, the mighty Maker, died
For man, the creature's sin.

4 Thus might I hide my blushing face
While his dear cross appears;
Dissolve my heart in thankfulness,
And melt mine eyes to tears.

5 But drops of grief can ne'er repay
The debt of love I owe;
Here, Lord, I give myself away,—
'Tis all that I can do.

At the Cross.

R. Kelso Carter.   From "Songs of Perfect Love," by per.

1. O Je - sus, Lord, thy dy - ing love Hath pierced my con- trite heart;
2. A - mid the night of sin and death Thy light hath filled my soul;
3. I kiss thy feet, I clasp thy hand, I touch thy bleeding side;
4. My Lord, my light, my strength, my all, I count my gain but loss;

Cho.—At the cross, at the cross, where I first saw the light,
And the burden of my heart rolled away,

Now take my life, and let me prove How dear to me thou art.
To me thy lov - ing voice now saith, Thy faith hath made thee whole.
Oh, let me here for - ev - er stand, Where thou wast cru - ci - fied.
For - ev - er let thy love enthrall, And keep me at the cross.

It was there by faith I received my sight, And now I am happy night and day!

117 P. Doddridge.
Happy Day.

English Melody.

1. { O happy day, that fixed my choice On thee, my Saviour and my God!
Well may this glowing heart rejoice, And tell its raptures all abroad. } Happy

Fine.   D.S.

day, happy day,   { He taught me how to watch and pray,
When Jesus washed my sins away!   And live rejoicing ev'ry day.

2 O happy bond, that seals my vows
   To him who merits all my love!
Let cheerful anthems fill his house,
   While to that sacred shrine I move.

3 'Tis done! the great transaction's done!
   I am my Lord's, and he is mine:
He drew me, and I followed on,
   Charmed to confess that voice divine.

4 Now rest, my long-divided heart;
   Fixed on this blissful center, rest;
Nor ever from thy Lord depart;
   With him of every good possessed.

5 High heav'n that heard the solemn vow,
   That vow renewed shall daily hear,
Till in life's latest hour I bow,
   And bless in death a bond so dear.

118 It is Good to be Here.

Rev. I. N. Wilson

Jno. R. Sweney, by per.

1. { While we bow in thy name, Oh, meet us a-gain, Fill our
    { May the Spir - it of grace, And the smiles of thy face, Gent - ly

D. S.—light streaming down makes the pathway all clear, It is

Fine. REFRAIN.

hearts with the light of thy love; }
fall on us now from a - bove. } It is good to be here, it is

good for us, Lord, to be here.

D. S.

good to be here, Thy perfect love now drives a-way all our fear, And

2 Our souls long for thee;
Oh, may we now see
A sin-cleansing blood-wave appear;
And feel, as it rolls
In power o'er our souls,
It is good for us, Lord, to be here.

3 Thou art with us, we know;
We feel the sweet flow   [tide;
Of the sin-cleansing wave's gladd'ning
We are washed from our sin,
Made all holy within,
And in Jesus we sweetly abide.

Copyright, 1879, by Jno. R. Sweney.

DO RE MI FA SO LA SI

119   OH, HOW HAPPY ARE THEY.   Tune and Chorus above.

Oh, how happy are they
Who the Saviour obey,
And have laid up their treasures above;
Tongue can never express
The sweet comfort and peace
Of a soul in its earliest love.

2 That sweet comfort was mine,
When the favor divine
I received thro' the blood of the Lamb;
When my heart first believed,
What a joy I received—
What a heaven in Jesus' name!

3 'Twas a heaven below
My Redeemer to know,
And the angels could do nothing more
Than to fall at his feet,
And the story repeat,
And the Lover of sinners adore.

4 Jesus, all the day long,
Was my joy and my song;
Oh, that all his salvation might see;
He hath loved me, I cried,
He hath suffered and died,
To r.. even rebels like me.

Till He Come.

"For yet a little while and he that shall come will come, and will not tarry."—Heb. x. 37.

Rev. Ed H. Bickersteth.

Dr. Lowell Mason.

Fine.

1. "Till he come!" Oh, let the words Lin-ger on the trembling chords;
D. C.—Let us think how heaven and home Lie beyond that "Till he come!"
2. When the wea-ry ones we love En-ter on that rest a-bove,
D. C.—Hush! be ev-'ry murmur dumb, It is on-ly "Till he come!"

D. C.

Let the "lit-tle while" be-tween In their golden light be seen;
When the words of love and cheer Fall no long-er on our ear,

3 Clouds and darkness round us press;
Would we have one sorrow less?
All the sharpness of the cross,
All that tells the world is loss,
Death, and darkness, and the tomb,
Pain us only "Till he come!"

4 See, the feast of love is spread.
Drink the wine and eat the bread;
Sweet memorials, till the Lord
Call us round his heavenly board.
Some from earth, from glory some,
Severed only "Till he come!"

121 To-Day the Saviour Calls.

Samuel Francis Smith.

Dr. Lowell Mason.

1 To-day the Saviour calls;
Ye wand'rers, come;
O ye benighted souls,
Why longer roam?

2 To-day the Saviour calls;
Oh, hear him now;
Within these sacred walls
To Jesus bow.

3 To-day the Saviour calls;
For refuge fly;
The storm of justice falls,
And death is nigh.

4 The Spirit calls to-day;
Yield to his power,
Oh, grieve him not away,
'Ti- mercy's hour.

122 Must Jesus Bear the Cross.

Thomas Shepherd. Alt.　　　　　　　　　Tune, MAITLAND. C. M.

1. Must Je - sus bear the cross a - lone, And all the world go free?

No, there's a cross for ev - 'ry one, And there's a cross for me.

2 How happy are the saints above,
　Who once went sorrowing here!
　But now they taste unmingled love,
　And joy without a tear.

3 The consecrated cross I'll bear,
　Till death shall set me free;
　And then go home my crown to wear,
　For there's a crown for me.

123 C. J. B. A Sinner like Me.

Chas. J. Butler.

1. I was once far away from the Saviour, And as vile as a sinner could be,

I wondered if Christ the Redeemer Could save a poor sinner like me.

2 I wandered on in the darkness,
　Not a ray of light could I see, [ness,
　And the thought filled my heart with sad-
　There's no hope for a sinner like me.

3 I then fully trusted in Jesus,
　And oh, what a joy came to me;
　My heart was filled with his praises,
　For saving a sinner like me.

4 No longer in darkness I'm walking,
　For the light is now shining on me,
　And now unto others I'm telling,
　How he saved a poor sinner like me.

5 And when life's journey is over,
　And I the dear Saviour shall see,
　I'll praise him for ever and ever.
　For saving a sinner like me.

Copyright, 1881, by John J. Hood,

124 Onward, Christian Soldiers!

SABINE BARING-GOULD.   Tune, ONWARD. 6, 5.

1. Onward, Christian soldiers! Marching as to war, With the cross of Jesus
2. At the sign of triumph Satan's host doth flee; On, then, Christian soldiers,
3. Like a mighty army Moves the Church of God; Brothers, we are treading

Go-ing on be-fore. Christ, the royal Mas - ter, Leads against the foe;
On to vic - to - ry! Hell's foundations qiv - er At the shout of praise;
Where the saints have trod; We are not di - vid - ed, All one bo-dy we,

CHORUS.

Forward into bat - tle, See, his banners go!   Onward, Christian soldiers!
Brothers, lift your voices, Loud your anthems raise.
One in hope and doctrine, One in chari - ty.

Marching as to war, With the cross of Je - sus Going on be-fore.

4 Crowns and thrones may perish,
   Kingdoms rise and wane,
  But the Church of Jesus
   Constant will remain;
  Gates of hell can never
   'Gainst that Church prevail
  We have Christ's own promise,
   And that cannot fai'.

5 Onward, then, ye people!
   Join our happy throng,
  Blend with ours your voices
   In the triumph-song;
  Glory, laud, and honor
   Unto Christ the King,
  This through countless ages
   Men and angels sing.

125 Come to Jesus.

1. Come to Je - sus, Come to Je - sus, Come to Je - sus just now, Just
now come to Jesus, Come to Je - sus just now.

2 He will save you, etc.
3 He is able, etc.   •
4 He is willing, etc.
5 He is waiting, etc.
6 O believe him, etc.
7 He will bless you, etc.

126 Abide with Me.

HENRY F. LYTE.
Tune, EVENTIDE. 10s.

1. Abide with me! fast falls the eventide, The darkness deepens–Lord, with me abide!
When other helpers fail, and comforts flee, Help of the helpless, oh, abide with me.

2 Swift to its close ebbs out life's little day;
Earth's joys grow dim, its glories pass away;
Change and decay in all around I see;
O thou, who changest not, abide with me!

3 I need thy presence every passing hour;
What but thy grace can foil the tempter's power?
Who, like thyself, my guide and stay can be?
Through cloud and sunshine, Lord, abide with me!

4 I fear no foe, with thee at hand to bless;
Ills have no weight, and tears no bitterness;
Where is death's sting? where, grave, thy victory?
I triumph still, if thou abide with me.

5 Hold thou thy cross before my closing eyes;
Shine through the gloom and point me to the skies;
Heaven's morning breaks, and earth's vain shadows flee;
In life, in death, O Lord, abide with me!

The Lord's Garden.

Tune, GARDEN.

1 The Lord into his garden comes,
The spices yield their rich perfumes, The lilies grow and thrive, The lilies grow and thrive; Refreshing showers of grace divine From Jesus flow to ev-'ry vine, And make the dead revive, And make the dead revive.

2 O that this dry and barren ground
In springs of water may abound,—
A fruitful soil become;
The desert blossoms like the rose,
When Jesus conquers all his foes,
And makes his people one.

3 Come, brethren, you that love the Lord,
Who taste the sweetness of his word,
In Jesus' ways go on;
Our troubles and our trials here,
Will only make us richer there,
When we arrive at home.

128

REGINALD HEBER.

Holy, holy, holy.

Tune, NICEA. 11, 12, 10.

1. Ho-ly, ho-ly, ho - ly, Lord God Almight-y! Ear-ly in the
2. Ho-ly, ho-ly, ho - ly! all the saints adore thee, Casting down their
3. Ho-ly, ho-ly, ho - ly! tho' the darkness hide thee, Tho' the eye of
4. Ho-ly, ho-ly, ho - ly. Lord God Almight-y! All thy works shall

morn - ing our song shall rise to thee; Ho - ly, ho - ly, ho - ly,
gold- en crowns around the glas - sy sea; Cher - u- bim and seraphim
sin - ful man thy glo - ry may not see; On - ly thou art ho - ly!
praise thy name, in earth, and sky, and sea; Ho - ly, ho - ly, ho - ly,

mer - ci-ful and might-y, God in Three Persons, blessed Trin - i - ty!
falling down before thee, Which wert, and art, and evermore shalt be.
there is none be-side thee, Per- feet in power, in love, and pur - i - ty.
mer - ci-ful and might-y, God in Three Persons, blessed Trin - i - ty!

129 My Faith Looks Up to Thee.

RAY PALMER.   L. MASON.

1 My faith looks up to thee,
Thou Lamb of Calvary,
   Saviour divine!
Now hear me while I pray;
Take all my guilt away;
Oh, let me from this day
   Be wholly thine!

2 May thy rich grace impart
Strength to my fainting heart,
   My zeal inspire!

As thou hast died for me,
Oh, may my love to thee
Pure, warm, and changeless be—
   A living fire!

3 While life's dark maze I tread,
And griefs around me spread,
   Be thou my guide;
Bid darkness turn to day,
Wipe sorrow's tears away,
Nor let me ever stray
   From thee aside!

4 When ends life's transient dream,
When death's cold sullen stream
   Shall o'er me roll,
Blest Saviour! then, in love,
Fear and distrust remove;
Oh, bear me safe above—
   A ransomed soul!

When shall We all Meet again?

Arr. by L. H. EDMUNDS.

Adapted and arr. by WM. J. KIRKPATRICK.

1. When shall we all meet a - gain? When shall we all meet a - gain?
2. Soon we shall all meet a - gain, Soon we shall all meet a - gain,
3. There we shall all Je - sus see, There we shall all Je - sus see,
4. There we may wear starry crowns, There we may wear star - ry crowns

When shall we all meet a - gain? If not on earth, in heav- en
Soon we shall all meet a - gain, If not on earth, in heav- en
There we shall all Je - sus see, If not on earth, in heav- en
There we may wear starry crowns, Tho' not on earth, in heav- en

Shall we all meet a - gain?
We shall all meet a - gain.
We shall all Je - sus see.
We may all wear bright crowns.

5 ‖: There we shall meet friends we love, :‖
   When we get home to heaven
   We shall meet friends we love.

6 ‖: There we shall *never* part again, :‖
   When we get home to heaven
   We shall *never* part again.

7 ‖: There we shall *never* say good-by, :‖
   When we get home to heaven
   We shall *never* say good-by.

Copyright, 1891, by Wm. J. Kirkpatrick.

131

The Golden Key.

"Prayer is the key to unlock the door, and the bolt to shut in the night."

JNO. R. SWENEY.

1. Prayer is the key For the bending knee To open the morn's first hours;
2. Not a soul so sad, Nor a heart so glad When cometh the shades of night,
3. Take the golden key In your hand and see, As the night tide drifts away,

See the incense rise To the starry skies, Like per-fume from the flow'rs.
But the daybreak song Will the joy prolong, And some darkness turn to light.
How its blessed hold Is a crown of gold, Thro' the weary hours of day.

4 When the shadows fall,
  And the vesper call
Is sobbing its low refrain,
  'Tis a garland sweet
  To the toil dent feet,
And an antidote for pain

5 Soon the year's dark door
  Shall be shut no more:
Life's tears shall be wiped away,
  As the pearl gates swing,
  And the gold harps ring,
And the sun unsheathe for aye.

Copyright, 1875, by John J. Hood.

132 Jesus, I Come to Thee.

FANNY J. CROSBY. WM. J. KIRKPATRICK.

1. Je - sus, I come to thee, Longing for rest; Fold thou thy
2. Je - sus, I come to thee, Hear thou my cry; Save, or I
3. Now let the roll- ing waves Bend to thy will, Say to the
4. Swiftly the part- ing clouds Fade from my sight; Yon- der thy

CHORUS.

wea - ry child Safe to thy breast. Rocked on a storm- y sea,
per - ish, Lord, Save, or I die.
troubled deep, Peace, peace, be still.
bow ap- pears, Love - ly and bright.

Oh, be not far from me. Lord, let me cling to thee, On - ly to thee.

Copyright, 1884, by John J. Hood.

Jesus will Meet You There.

W. L. K.

W. Lewis Kane.

1. Come to Calv'ry's mount to-day, Je-sus will meet you there;
Look and live without de-lay, Je-sus will meet you there.

CHORUS.

Come to Jesus, Don't stay away, my friend; Come to Jesus, Dont stay away.

2 Rest beneath the hallowed cross,
Jesus will meet you there;
Saving mercy gained for loss,
Jesus will meet you there.

8 Come and join his faithful band,
Jesus will meet you there;
Take his mighty, helping hand,
Jesus will meet you there.

4 At the blessed mercy seat,
Jesus will meet you there;
Come with this assurance sweet,
Jesus will meet you there.

5 You'll find rest in heaven at last,
Jesus will meet you there;
And be happy with the blest,
Jesus will meet you there.

134 Cowper. **Glorious Fountain.**

T. C. O'Kane.
By per.

1. There is a fountain filled with blood, filled with blood, filled with blood,
And sinners, plung'd beneath that flood, beneath that flood, beneath that flood,

2. The dy-ing thief rejoiced to see, rejoiced to see, rejoiced to see,
And there may I, tho' vile as he, tho' vile as he, tho' vile as he,

There is a fountain filled with blood. Drawn from Immanuel's veins,
And sinners, plung'd beneath that flood. Lose all their guilty stains.

The dy-ing thief rejoiced to see That fountain in his day,
And there may I, tho' vile as he, Wash all my sins a-way.

Glorious Fountain.—CONCLUDED.

CHORUS.

Oh, glo-ri-ous fountain! Here will I stay, And in thee ev-er

Wash my sins a-way.

3 Thou dying Lamb, ‖: thy precious blood
Shall never lose its power,
Till all the ransomed ‖: Church of God :
Are saved, to sin no more.

4 E'er since by faith ‖: I saw the stream :‖
Thy flowing wounds supply,
Redeeming love ‖: has been my theme, :‖
And shall be till I die.

135 Glory to His Name.

Rev. E. A. Hoffman.   *"I will glorify thy name forevermore."*   Rev. J. H. Stocktor

1. Down at the cross where my Saviour died, Down where for cleansing from
2. I am so wondrously saved from sin, Je-sus so sweetly a-
3. Oh, precious fountain, that saves from sin! I am so glad I have
4. Come to this fountain, so rich and sweet; Cast thy poor soul at the

sin I cried; There to my heart was the blood ap-plied; Glo-ry to his
bides within; There at the cross where he took me in; Glo-ry to his
entered in; There Jesus saves me and keeps me clean; Glo-ry to his
Saviour's feet; Plunge in to-day, and be made complete; Glo-ry to his

D.S.—There to my heart was the blood applied; Glo-ry to his

Fine. CHORUS.   *D.S.*

name. Glo-ry to his name, Glo-ry to his name;

By permission.

Jesus is Mine!

"My beloved is mine."—S of Sol. ii. 16.

Mrs. Catharine J. Bonar.   T. E. Perkins. By per.

1. Fade, fade, each earth-ly joy, Je-sus is mine! Break, ev-'ry
2. Tempt not my soul a-way, Je-sus is mine! Here would I
3. Fare-well, ye dreams of night, Je-sus is mine! Lost in this
4. Fare-well, mor-tal-i-ty, Je-sus is mine! Wel-come, e-

ten-der tie, Je-sus is mine! Dark is the wil-derness,
ev-er stay, Je-sus is mine! Per-ish-ing things of clay,
dawn-ing light, Je-sus is mine! All that my soul has tried
ter-ni-ty, Je-sus is mine! Wel-come, O loved and blest,

Earth has no resting place, Je-sus alone can bless, Je-sus is mine!
Born but for one brief day, Pass from my heart away, Je-sus is mine!
Left but a dismal void, Je-sus has sat-is-fied, Je-sus is mine!
Welcome, sweet scenes of rest, Welcome, my Saviour's breast, Jesus is mine!

137 I'll Live for Him.

C. R. Dunbar.

1. My life, my love I give to thee, Thou Lamb of God, who died for me,
2. I now believe thou dost receive, For thou hast died that I might live;
3. Oh, thou who died on Cal-va-ry, To save my soul and make me free.

Cho.—I'll live for him who died for me, How happy then my life shall be!

Copyright of R. E. Hudson, used by per.

I'll Live for Him.—CONCLUDED.

D. C.

Oh, may I ev - er faith-ful be, My Sav-iour and my God!
And now henceforth I'll trust in thee, My Sav-iour and my God!
I con - se-crate my life to thee, My Sav-iour and my God!

I'll live for him who died for me, My Sav-iour and my God!

---

138 H. BONAR. ## What a Friend. C. C. CONVERSE. By per.

1. What a Friend we have in Je - sus, All our sins and griefs to bear!

Fine.

What a priv - i - lege to car - ry Ev - 'rything to God in prayer!

D.S.—All because we do not car - ry Ev - 'rything to God in prayer!

D. S.

O what peace we oft-en for - feit, O what needless pain we bear,

2 Have we trials and temptations?
   Is there trouble anywhere?
We should never be discouraged,
   Take it to the Lord in prayer.
Can we find a friend so faithful
   Who will all our sorrows share?
Jesus knows our every weakness,
   Take it to the Lord in prayer.

3 Are we weak and heavy laden,
   Cumbered with a load of care?-
Precious Saviour, still our refuge,—
   Take it to the Lord in prayer.
Do thy friends despise, forsake thee?
   Take it to the Lord in prayer;
In his arms he'll take and shield thee,
   Thou wilt find a solace there.

I'll be There.

Isaac Watts.   Adapted by Wm. J. Kirkpatrick.

1. There is a land of pure delight, Where saints immor - tal reign ;
   In - fi - nite day ex - cludes the night, And pleasures ban - ish pain.

2. There ev - er-last-ing spring abides, And nev - er-with'ring flowers;
   Death, like a narrow sea, divides This heavenly land from ours.

REFRAIN.

I'll be there, I'll be there, When the first trumpet sounds I'll be there.

I'll be there,

I'll be there, I'll be there, When the first trumpet sounds I'll be there.

3 Sweet fields beyond the swelling flood
  Stand dressed in living green ;
  So to the Jews old Canaan stood,
  While Jordan rolled between.

4 Could we but climb where Moses stood,
  And view the landscape o'er. [flood
  Not Jordan's stream, nor death's cold
  Should fright us from the shore.

Copyright, 1887, by Wm. J. Kirkpatrick.

140   Praise, Praise His Name.

Fanny J. Crosby.   Jno. R. Sweney.

1. On the desert mountain straying, Far, far from home. Heard I there a sweet voice,
2. At a throne of mercy kneeling, Sad and oppressed, Came that voice, to me re-
3. Oft I heard that voice repeating, "I am the way, Tarry not, the hours are
4. When from glory unto glory My flight shall be, Still I'll sing the precious

Praise, Praise His Name.—CONCLUDED.

CHORUS.

saying, Why wilt thou roam? 'Twas my blessed Lord that sought me, Out of
vealing Hope, life, and rest.
fleeting, Come, come to-day."
sto - ry, Saviour, of thee.

sin to grace he brought me, Oh, the glad, new song he taught me,—Praise, praise his
[name!

Copyright, 1801, by John R. Sweney.

141   Just as I Am.

CHARLOTTE ELLIOTT.   Tune, HAMBURG. L. M.

1. Just as I am, with - out one plea, But that thy blood was shed for me,
2. Just as I am, and wait- ing not To rid my soul of one dark blot,

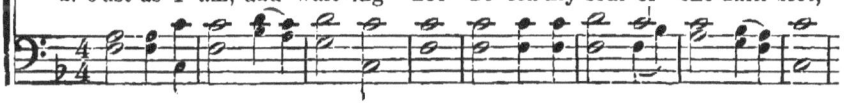

And that thou bid'st me come to thee, O Lamb of God, I come! I come!
To thee, whose blood can cleanse each spot, O Lamb of God, I come! I come!

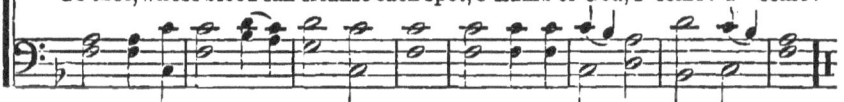

3 Just as I am, though tossed about
  With many a conflict, many a doubt,
  Fightings within, and fears without,
  O Lamb of God, I come! I come!

4 Just as I am—poor, wretched, blind;
  Sight, riches, healing of the mind,
  Yea, all I need, in thee to find,
  O Lamb of God, I come! I come!

5 Just as I am—thou wilt receive,
  Wilt welcome, pardon, cleanse, relieve,
  Because thy promise I believe,
  O Lamb of God, I come! I come!

6 Just as I am—thy love unknown
  Hath broken every barrier down;
  Now to be thine, yea, thine alone,
  O Lamb of God, I come! come!

125

142 He Leadeth Me!

1 HE leadeth me! O blessed thought!
O words with heavenly comfort fraught!
Whate'er I do, where'er I be,
Still 'tis God's hand that leadeth me.

Cho.—He leadeth me, he leadeth me,
By his own hand he leadeth me:
His faithful follower I would be,
For by his hand he leadeth me.

2 Sometimes 'mid scenes of deepest gloom,
Sometimes where Eden's bowers bloom,
By waters still, o'er troubled sea,—
Still 'tis his hand that leadeth me!

3 Lord, I would clasp thy hand in mine,
Nor ever murmur nor repine,
Content, whatever lot I see,
Since 'tis my God that leadeth me!

143 Come, thou Fount.

1 Come, thou Fount of every blessing,
Tune my heart to sing thy grace;
Streams of mercy, never ceasing,
Call for songs of loudest praise;
Teach me some melodious sonnet,
Sung by flaming tongues above;
Praise the mount—I'm fixed upon it!
Mount of thy redeeming love.

2 Here I raise my Ebenezer,
Hither by thy help I'm come;
And I hope, by thy good pleasure,
Safely to arrive at home.
Jesus sought me when a stranger,
Wandering from the fold of God;
He, to rescue me from danger,
Interposed his precious blood.

3 Oh, to grace how great a debtor
Daily I'm constrained to be!
Let thy goodness, like a fetter,
Bind my wandering heart to thee;
Prone to wander, Lord, I feel it—
Prone to leave the God I love—
Here's my heart, oh, take and seal it,
Seal it for thy courts above.

144 Blest be the tie.

1 BLEST be the tie that binds
Our hearts in Christian love;
The fellowship of kindred minds
Is like to that above.

2 Before our Father's throne
We pour our ardent prayers;
Our fears, our hopes, our aims are one,
Our comforts and our cares.

3 We share our mutual woes,
Our mutual burdens bear;
And often for each other flows
The sympathising tear.

4 When we asunder part
It gives us inward pain;
But we shall still be joined in heart,
And hope to meet again.

145 Nearer to Thee.

1 NEARER, my God, to thee!
Nearer to thee,
E'en though it be a cross
That raiseth me;
Still all my song shall be,
Nearer, my God, to thee,
Nearer to thee!

2 Though like the wanderer,
The sun gone down,
Darkness be over me,
My rest a stone,
Yet in my dreams I'd be,
Nearer, my God, to thee,
Nearer to thee!

3 There let the way appear
Steps unto heaven;
All that thou sendest me
In mercy given;
Angels to beckon me
Nearer, my God, to thee,
Nearer to thee!

146 Sweet Hour of Prayer.

1 Sweet hour of prayer, sweet hour of prayer,
That calls me from a world of care,
And bids me at my Father's throne
Make all my wants and wishes known!
In seasons of distress and grief
My soul has often found relief,
And oft escaped the tempter's snare
By thy return, sweet hour of prayer.

2 Sweet hour of prayer, sweet hour of prayer,
Thy wings shall my petition bear
To him, whose truth and faithfulness
Engage the waiting soul to bless:
And since he bids me seek his face,
Believe his word, and trust his grace,
I'll cast on him my every care,
And wait for thee, sweet hour of prayer.

Ariel. C. P. M.

Arr. by LOWELL MASON.

147 O Love Divine.

1 O LOVE divine, how sweet thou art!
When shall I find my willing heart
All taken up by thee?
I thirst, I faint, I die to prove
The greatness of redeeming love,
The love of Christ to me.

2 Stronger his love than death or hell;
Its riches are unsearchable;
The first-born sons of light
Desire in vain its depths to see;
They cannot reach the mystery,
The length, the breadth, the height.

3 God only knows the love of God;
O that it now were shed abroad
In this poor stony heart!
For love I sigh, for love I pine;
This only portion, Lord, be mine;
Be mine this better part.

4 O that I could forever sit
With Mary at the Master's feet!
Be this my happy choice;
My only care, delight, and bliss,
My joy, my heaven on earth, be this,
To hear the Bridegroom's voice.

5 O that I could, with favored John,
Recline my weary head upon
The dear Redeemer's breast!

From care, and sin, and sorrow free,
Give me, O Lord, to find in thee
My everlasting rest.

148 O could I Speak.

1 O COULD I speak the matchless worth,
O could I sound the glories forth,
Which in my Saviour shine,
I'd soar and touch the heavenly strings,
And vie with Gabriel while he sings
In notes almost divine.

2 I'd sing the precious blood he spilt,
My ransom from the dreadful guilt
Of sin, and wrath divine;
I'd sing his glorious righteousness,
In which all-perfect, heavenly dress
My soul shall ever shine.

3 I'd sing the characters he bears,
And all the forms of love he wears,
Exalted on his throne;
In loftiest songs of sweetest praise,
I would to everlasting days
Make all his glories known.

4 Well, the delightful day will come
When my dear Lord will bring me
And I shall see his face;   [home,
Then with my Saviour, Brother, Friend,
A blest eternity I'll spend,
Triumphant in his grace,

Forest. L. M.

149   O that my load of sin were gone.   L. M.

1 O that my load of sin were gone!
O that I could at last submit
At Jesus' feet to lay it down—
To lay my soul at Jesus' feet!

2 Rest for my soul I long to find:
Saviour of all, if mine thou art,
Give me thy meek and lowly mind,
And stamp thine image on my heart.

3 Break off the yoke of inbred sin,
And fully set my spirit free;

I cannot rest till pure within,
Till I am wholly lost in thee.

4 Fain would I learn of thee, my God,
Thy light and easy burden prove,
The cross all stained with hallowed blood,
The labor of thy dying love.

5 I would, but thou must give the power;
My heart from every sin release;
Bring near, bring near the joyful hour,
And fill me with thy perfect peace.

—Chas. Wesley.

150   Lord, I am Thine.   L. M.

1 Lord, I am thine, entirely thine,
Purchased and saved by blood divine;
With full consent thine would I be,
And own thy sovereign right in me.

2 Thine would I live, thine would I die,
Be thine through all eternity;
The vow is past, beyond repeal,
And now I set the solemn seal.

3 Here, at that cross where flows the blood
That bought my guilty soul for God,
Thee, my new Master now I call,
And consecrate to thee my all.

4 Do thou assist a feeble worm
The great engagement to perform;
Thy grace can full assistance lend,
And on that grace I dare depend.

—Samuel Davies

151   I thirst, Thou wounded Lamb of God.   L. M.

1 I thirst, thou wounded Lamb of God,
To wash me in thy cleansing blood;
To dwell within thy wounds; then pain
Is sweet, and life or death is gain.

2 Take my poor heart, and let it be
Forever closed to all but thee:
Seal thou my breast, and let me wear
That pledge of love forever there.

3 How blest are they who still abide
Close sheltered in thy bleeding side!
Who thence their life and strength derive,
And by thee move, and in thee live.

4 What are our works but sin and death
Till thou thy quickening Spirit breathe?
Thou giv'st the power thy grace to move,
O wondrous grace! O wondrous love!

5 How can it be, thou heavenly King,
That thou shouldst us to glory bring?
Make slaves the partners of thy throne,
Decked with a never-fading crown?

6 Hence our hearts melt, our eyes o'erflow,
Our words are lost, nor will we know,
Nor will we think of aught beside,
"My Lord, my Love is crucified."

—Nicolaus L. Zinzendorf.

152 Meet in the Morning.

H. E. BLAIR.   WM. J. KIRKPATRICK.

1. We are marching onward to the heavenly land, To meet each other in the morning;
2. We are trav'ling onward from a world of care, To meet each other in the morning;
3. We are trav'ling onward, and the way grows bright, We'll meet each other in, etc.,

We are pressing forward to the golden strand, Where joy will crown us in the morning.
Oh, the time is coming, we shall soon be there, And joy will crown us in the morning.
Where our friends are waiting, at the gate of life, And joy will crown us in the, etc.,

CHORUS.

In the morning, in the morning, We will gather with the faithful in the morning;

Where the night of sorrow shall be rolled away, And joy will crown us in the morning.

4 Where the hills are blooming on the other shore,
We'll meet each other in the morning!
Where the heart's deep longing will be felt no more,
And joy will crown us in the morning.

5 In the boundless rapture of a Saviours' love
We'll meet each other in the morning;
Then we'll sing his glory in the realms above,
And joy will crown us in the morning.

Copyright, 1888, by WM. J. KIRKPATRICK.

Redemption Songs—J

I will Shout His Praise in Glory.

P. H. DINGMAN.

JNO. R. SWENEY.

1. You ask what makes me happy, my heart so free from care, It is because my
2. I was a friendless wand'rer till Jesus took me in, My life was full of
3. I wish that ev'ry sinner before his throne would bow; He waits to bid them
4. I mean to live for Jesus while here on earth I stay, And when his voice shall

Sav - iour in mercy heard my prayer; He brought me out of darkness and
sor - row, my heart was full of sin; But when the blood so precious spoke
welcome, he longs to bless them now; If they but knew the rapture that
call me to realms of endless day, As one by one we gath - er, re-

now the light I see; O blessed, loving Saviour! to him the praise shall be.
pardon to my soul; Oh, blissful, blissful moment! 'twas joy beyond control.
in his love I see, They'd come and shout salvation, and sing his praise with me.
joicing on the shore, We'll shout his praise in glory, and sing forev - ermore.

CHORUS.

I will shout his praise in glo - ry, ... And we'll
So will I, so will I,

all sing halle - lu-jah in heav-en by and by; I will shout his praise in

Copyright, 1889, by Jno. R. Sweney.

I will Shout His Praise.—CONCLUDED.

glo - ry, . . . And we'll all sing hallelujah in heaven by and by.

So will I, so will I,

154 Hear and Answer Prayer.

FANNY J. CROSBY. WM. J. KIRKPATRICK.

1. I am pray - ing, bless- ed Sav - iour, To be more and more like thee;
2. I am pray - ing, bless- ed Sav - iour, For a faith so clear and bright
3. I am pray - ing to be hum- bled By the power of grace di - vine,
4. I am pray - ing, bless- ed Sav - iour, And my constant prayer shall be

I am pray - ing that thy Spir - it Like a dove may rest on me.
That its eye will see thy glo - ry Thro' the deep - est, dark- est night.
To be clothed up - on with meekness, And to have no will but thine.
For a per - fect con - se - cra - tion, That shall make me more like thee.

CHORUS.

Thou who know- est all my weak-ness, Thou who knowest all my care,

While I plead each precious promise, Hear, oh, hear and answer prayer.

Copyright, 1880, by WM. J. KIRKPATRICK.

Safe in the Glory Land.

James L. Black.　　　　　　　　　　　　　　Jno. R. Sweney.

1. In the good old way where the saints have gone, And the
2. In the good old way like the ransomed throng, Un - to
3. In the good old way with a stead - fast faith, In the
4. Tho' our feet must stand on the cold, cold brink Of the

King leads on be - fore us, We are travelling home to the
Zi - on now re - turn - ing, We are travelling home at the
bonds of love and un - ion, What a joy is ours for the
Jor - dan's storm - y riv - er, With the King we'll cross to the

heavenly hills, With the day-star shining o'er us.
King's command, And our lamps are trimm'd and burning.
King we see, And with him we hold communion.
oth - er side, And we'll sing his praise for-ev - er.

CHORUS.

Travelling home to the

man - sions fair, Crowns of re - joic - ing and life to wear;

O what a shout when we all get there, Safe in the glo - ry land!

Copyright, 1888, by Jno. R. Sweney.

156 Anywhere With Jesus.

JESSIE H. BROWN.   "I will trust and not be afraid." Isaiah xii. 2.   D. B. TOWNER.   By per.

1. An-ywhere with Je-sus I can safe-ly go, An-ywhere He
2. An-ywhere with Je-sus I am not a-lone, Other friends may
3. An-ywhere with Je-sus I can go to sleep, When the darkling

leads me in this world be-low. Anywhere without him, dearest
fail me, He is still my own. Tho' his hand may lead me o-ver
shadows round a-bout me creep; Knowing I shall waken nev-er

joys would fade, Anywhere with Je-sus I am not a-fraid.
drearest ways, Anywhere with Je-sus is a house of praise.
more to roam, Anywhere with Je-sus will be home, sweet home.

CHORUS.

An-y-where! an-y-where! Fear I can-not know.

An-y-where with Je-sus I can safe-ly go.

Copyright, 1887, by D. B. Towner.

133

My Spirit is Free.

W. A. S.   Rev. W. A. Spencer, D. D.

1. I fol - low the footsteps of Je - sus, my Lord, His Spir- it doth
2. A lep - er he found me, pol- lu - ted by sin, From which he a -
3. A cap-tive in woe to my pris - on of night, The Mas- ter hath
4. Proclaim it, 'tis done, full sal - va - tion is wrought For sin-ners from

lead me a - long; I walk in the pathway made plain by his word,
lone can set free; He spake, in his mer- cy, "I will, be thou clean,"
o - pen'd the door; Shout a- loud of deliv'rance, ye an- gels of light,
sor - row and woe; Sing a- loud of his grace who my pardon has bought,

REFRAIN.

And he fills all my soul with this song.   Glo - ry to God, my
And he in- stant-ly pur - i - fied me.
Praise his name, O my soul, ev - er - more.
For his blood washes whit- er than snow.

spir - it is free, Glo - ry to God, he pur - i - fies me; I'm

walking the thorn-path, but joyful I'll be While following Jesus, my Lord.

By permission.

Stepping in the Light.

L. H. Edmunds.   W. J. Kirkpatrick.

1. Trying to walk in the steps of the Saviour, Trying to follow our
2. Pressing more closely to him who is leading, When we are tempted to
3. Walking in footsteps of gen - tle forbearance, Footsteps of faithfulness,
4. Trying to walk in the steps of the Saviour, Upward, still upward we'll

Saviour and King; Shaping our lives by his blessed ex- am - ple,
turn from the way; Trusting the arm that is strong to defend us,
mer - cy, and love, Looking to him for the grace free- ly promised,
fol - low our Guide, When we shall see him, "the King in his beauty,"

CHORUS.

Happy, how happy, the songs that we bring. How beautiful to walk in the
Happy, how happy, our praises each day.
Happy, how happy, our journey above.
Happy, how happy, our place at his side.

steps of the Saviour, Stepping in the light, Stepping in the light; How

beautiful to walk in the steps of the Saviour, Led in paths of light.

Copyright, 1890, by Wm. J. Kirkpatrick.

The Firm Foundation.

GEORGE KEITH.

Tune, PORTUGUESE HYMN.

1. How firm a foundation, ye saints of the Lord, Is laid for your
2. "Fear not, I am with thee, O be not dismayed, For I am thy
3. "When thro' the deep waters I call thee to go, The riv-ers of
4. "When thro' fie-ry tri-als thy path-way shall lie, My grace all suf -

faith in his ex-cel-lent word ' What more can he say, than to
God, I will still give thee aid; I'll strengthen thee, help thee, and
sor-row shall not o-ver-flow; For I will be with thee thy
fi-cient, shall be thy sup-ply, The flame shall not hurt thee; I

you he hath said, To you, who for re-fuge to Je-sus have
cause thee to stand, Up-held by my gracious, om-ni-po-tent
tri-als to bless, And sanc-ti-fy to thee thy deepest dis-
on-ly de-sign Thy dross to consume, and thy gold to re-

fled? To you, who for re-fuge to Je-sus have fled?
hand, Up-held by my gracious, om-ni-po-tent hand.
tress, And sanc-ti-fy to thee thy deep-est dis-tress.
fine, Thy dross to consume, and thy gold to re-fine.

6 "E'en down to old age all my people
shall prove   [love;
My sovereign, eternal, unchangeable
And when hoary hairs shall their tem-
ples adorn,   [be borne.
Like lambs they shall still in my bosom

6 "The soul that on Jesus hath leaned
for repose,
I will not, I will not desert to his foes;
That soul, though all hell should en-
deavor to shake,
I'll never, no never, no never forsake!"

The Haven of Rest.

H. L. Gilmour.   Geo. D. Moore.

1. My soul in sad ex - ile was out on life's sea, So
2. I yield - ed my - self to his ten - der embrace, And
3. The song of my soul, since the Lord made me whole, Has
4. How pre - cious the thought that we all may re - cline, Like
5. Oh, come to the Sav - iour, he pa - tient- ly waits To

burdened with sin, and dis - trest, Till I heard a sweet voice saying,
faith taking hold of the word, My fetters fell off, and I
been the OLD STORY so blest Of Jesus, who'll save who-so-
John the be- lov - ed and blest, On Jesus' strong arm, where no
save by his power di - vine; Come, anchor your soul in the

D. S.—The tempest may sweep o'er the

Fine.

make me your choice; And I entered the "Ha - ven of Rest!"
anchored my soul; The ha - ven of rest is my Lord.
ev - er will have A home in the "Ha - ven of Rest!"
tem - pest can harm,— Se - cure in the "Ha - ven of Rest!"
ha - ven of rest, And say, "my Be - lov - ed is mine."

wild, stormy deep, In Je - sus I'm safe ev - er - more.

CHORUS.   D. S.

I've anchored my soul in the haven of rest, I'll sail the wide seas no more;

Copyright, 1889, by John J. Hood

Tell It Out with Gladness.

Fanny J. Crosby.

Jno. R. Sweney.

Moderato.

1. Are you hap-py in the Lord, Tell it out with gladness; Are you
2. Are you walking in the light, Tell it out with gladness; Is your
3. Do you love the place of prayer, Tell it out with gladness; Do you

trusting in his word, Tell it out with gladness; If a Saviour's love you feel,
hope of glory bright, Tell it out with gladness; Have you perfect peace within,
find a blessing there, Tell it out with gladness; While your thoughts on Jesus dwell,

Can your soul its power conceal? To the world your joy reveal, Tell it
Are you try-ing still to win Constant victory o - ver sin, Tell it
Does your soul with rapture swell? Can you say that all is well? Tell it

CHORUS.

out with gladness. Tell it out, tell it out, tell it out with gladness, Tell it

out, tell it out, tell it out with gladness, Tell the world . . . the joy you

world the joy you feel, tell the

Copyright, 1889, by Jno. R. Sweney.

feel,   Tell it out, tell it out with glad - ness.

world the joy you feel,

162   All for Jesus.

MARY D. JAMES.   JNO. R. SWENEY

1. All for Je - sus! all for Je - sus! All my being's ransomed powers:
2. Let my hands perform his bidding, Let my feet run in his ways—
3. Worldlings prize their gems of beauty, Cling to gild- ed toys of dust,
4. Since my eyes were fixed on Je- sus, I've lost sight of all be- sides;
5. Oh, what wonder! how a - mazing! Je - sus, glorious King of kings—

Fine.

All my thoughts, and words, and doings, All my days, and all my hours.
Let my eyes see Je - sus on - ly, Let my lips speak forth his praise.
Boast of wealth, and fame, and pleasure: On - ly Je - sus will I trust.
So enchained my spir- it's vis- ion, Looking at the Cru- ci - fied.
Deigns to call me his be - lov- ed, Lets me rest beneath his wings.

D.S.—All for Je - sus! blessed Je - sus! I am his. and he is mine.

CHORUS.   *D.S.*

All for Je- sus! blessed Je - sus! All for Je- sus, gladly I re- sign;

Copyright, 1891, by Jno. R. Sweney.

163   I'm Happy, so Happy!

LIZZIE EDWARDS.   JNO. R. SWENEY.

1.   I'm happy, so happy! no words can express The joy and the comfort I see;
2.   I'm happy, so happy! while trusting in him Whose presence o'ershadows my way;
3.   My love may be tested, my faith may be tried, The depth of its fervor to prove,
4. O blessed Redeemer, some day I shall stand O'erwhelmed with the light of thy face,

For Jesus hath purchased, thro' infinite grace, A perfect salvation for me.
Who leadeth my soul by the river of peace, And giveth me strength as my day.
But welcome each trial, my Saviour designs The gold from the dross to remove.
Adoring forever, and shouting thy praise, Because thou hast saved me by grace.

CHORUS.

Saved, saved, oh, glo - ry to God! I feel the as - surance di - vine;

Saved, saved, oh, glo - ry to God! His Spir- it bears witness with mine.

Copyright, 1890, by Jno. R. Sweney.

164 **The Very Same Jesus.**

L. H. EDMUNDS.　　"This same Jesus."—Acts i : 11.　　WM. J. KIRKPATRICK.

1. Come, sinners, to the Liv- ing One, He's just the same Je- sus
2. Come, feast up- on the "living bread," He's just the same Je- sus
3. Come, tell him all your griefs and fears, He's just the same Je- sus
4. Come un - to him for clear- er light, He's just the same Je- sus

As when he raised the wid- ow's son, The ver - y same Je - sus.
As when the mul - ti - tudes he fed, The ver - y same Je - sus.
As when he shed those lov - ing tears, The ver - y same Je - sus.
As when he gave the blind their sight, The ver - y same Je - sus.

CHORUS.

The ver - y same Je - sus, The won- der work- ing Je - sus;

Oh, praise his name, he's just the same, The ver - y same Je - sus.

5 Calm 'midst the waves of trouble be,
He's just the same Jesus
As when he hushed the raging sea,
The very same Jesus.

6 Some day our raptured eyes shall see
He's just the same Jesus;
Oh, blessed day for you and me!
The very same Jesus.

Copyright, 1891, by Wm. J. Kirkpatrick.

Blessed be the Name.

W. H. CLARK.　　　　　　　　　　　Arranged by WM. J. KIRKPATRICK.

1. All praise to Him who reigns a-bove, In ma-jes-ty su-preme,
2. His name a-bove all names shall stand, Exalt-ed more and more,
3. Re-deem-er, Saviour, Friend of man Once ru-ined by the fall,
4. His name shall be the Counsel-lor, The might-y Prince of Peace,

Who gave his Son for man to die, That he might man re-deem.
At God the Father's own right hand, Where angel hosts a-dore.
Thou hast devised sal-vation's plan, For thou hast died for all.
Of all earth's kingdoms conquer-or, Whose reign shall never cease.

CHORUS.

Blessed be the name, blessed be the name, Blessed be the name of the Lord;

Blessed be the name, blessed be the name, Blessed be the name of the Lord.

5 The ransomed hosts to thee shall bring
　Their praise and homage meet;
With rapturous awe adore their King,
And worship at his feet.

6 Then shall we know as we are known,
　And in that world above
Forever sing around the throne
His everlasting love.

Copyright, 1888, by Wm. J. Kirkpatrick.

Looking Away to Jesus.

LIZZIE EDWARDS.

JNO. R. SWENEY.

1. There is joy within when faith is bright, Looking away to Je - sus;
2. Though our seed is sown in weakness here, Looking away to Je - sus;
3. There is joy within when love is warm, Looking away to Je - sus;
4. There's a bright reward for us in store, Looking away to Je - sus;

When the heart toils on from morn till night, Looking away to Je - sus.
We can sing our song of hap- py cheer, Looking away to Je - sus.
We can meet the wave and brave the storm, Looking away to Je - sus.
We shall meet with him and part no more, Looking away to Je - sus.

CHORUS.

Looking a - way, looking a- way, O work till the end we see;

Every soul we reclaim in the Saviour's name A star in our crown will be.

Copyright, 1891, by Jno. R. Sweney.

167. There's a Hand Held Out.

M. W. MORSE.   JNO. R. SWENEY.

1. There's a hand held out in pi-ty, There's a hand held out in love;   It will
2. Oh, how gently will it lead us!   Oh, how tender is its touch!   'Tis the
3. Yes, 'tis love to me, a sin-ner, Prompts this hand to reach so low,   Striving
4. Shall I, to this hand ex-tended,   Pay no heed as it in-vites?   Shall my

pi-lot to the ci-ty,   Where our Father dwells a-bove.
bless-ed hand of Je-sus;   We all need it, oh, so much!
thus to be the win-ner,   Ere I reap what I shall sow.
Sav-iour be of-fend-ed,   Give I not to him his rights?

CHORUS.

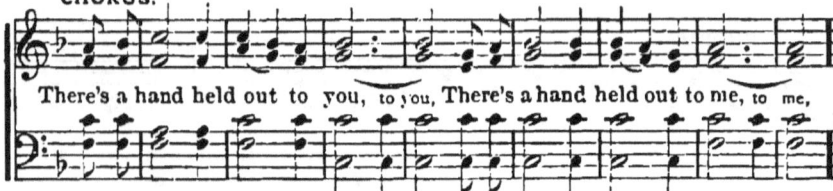

There's a hand held out to you, to you, There's a hand held out to me, to me,

There's a hand that will prove true, prove true, Whatev-er our lot shall be.

5 Nay, I would this proffered hand take,
  Knowing that it leads aright;
  Yes, I would this loving choice make;
  Trusting in his love and might.

6 Then, as hand in hand together
  With my Saviour, with my Friend,
  With my Christ, my Elder Brother,
  Let him lead till life shall end.

Copyright, 1889, by Jno. R. Sweney.

144

168   Only Believe.

EMMA M. JOHNSTON.   Mark v. 36.   WM. J. KIRKPATRICK.

1. Oh, why should we wres - tle with fears And doubts, which the
2. His word is as - sur - ance com - plete; Thy sins and thine
3. How ea - sy the terms of his grace: 'Tis on - ly to

Spir - it must grieve? And why should we languish in sor - row and tears,
i - dols now leave; Come, pleading his promise, and fall at his feet,
ask and re - ceive; The seal of his fav - or, the smile of his face,

CHORUS.

When there's nothing to do but be - lieve.   Be - lieve,   be-
Then you've nothing to do but be - lieve.
Are for those who will on - ly be - lieve.   Be - lieve, be-lieve,

lieve,   On - ly on Je - sus be - lieve; Sal - va - tion is

be - lieve,

wait-ing for you and for me, There is nothing to do but be - lieve.

Copyright, 1859, by WM. J. KIRKPATRICK.

The Everlasting Hymn.

E. E. Hewitt.   B. Hillyard Sweney.

1. Ho - ly, ho - ly, ho - ly; An - gel voi - ces sing - ing;
2. Ho - ly, ho - ly, ho - ly; Grandest mu - sic swell - ing;
3. Ho - ly, ho - ly, ho - ly; Come, let us a - dore him;

Ho - ly, ho - ly, ho - ly, Thro' high heav - en ring - ing.
Ho - ly, ho - ly, ho - ly, All sweet notes ex - cell - ing.
Ho - ly, ho - ly, ho - ly, Hum - bly bow be - fore him.

From that temple, pure and bright, Bathed in streams of crystal light,
Those who conquered by his might, Wearing now their crowns of light,
Wisdom, glo - ry, love and might, With the ser - a - phim u - nite

Hear the ev - er - lasting hymn, Ho - ly, ho - ly, ho - ly.
Join the ev - er - lasting hymn, Ho - ly, ho - ly, ho - ly.
In the ev - er - lasting hymn, Ho - ly, ho - ly, ho - ly.

Copyright, 1890, by Jno. R. Sweney.

146

Lead Me, Saviour.

F. M. D.   "For thy name's sake lead me, guide me."—Ps. xxxi. 3.   FRANK M. DAVIS.

With expression.

1. Saviour, lead me, lest I stray,   Gent- ly lead me all the way;
2. Thou the refuge of my soul   When life's stormy billows roll,
3. Saviour, lead me, then at last,   When the storm of life is past,

1. Sav - iour,   lead me, lest I stray, Gent - ly   lead me all the way;

I am safe when by thy side,   I would in thy love abide.
I am safe when thou art nigh,   All my hopes on thee rely.
To the land of endless day,   Where all tears are wiped away.

I am   safe when by thy side, I   would   in thy love abide.

CHORUS.

Lead me, lead me, Sav - iour, lead me, lest I stray; . . .

lest I stray;

rit. e dim.

Gently down the stream of time, Lead me, Saviour, all the way.

stream of time,   all the way.

From "Carols of Joy" by per.

Trust and Obey.

Rev. J. H. SAMMIS.   D. B. TOWNER.

1. When we walk with the Lord In the light of his word, What a glory he
2. Not a shadow can rise, Not a cloud in the skies, But his smile quickly
3. Not a burden we bear, Not a sorrow we share, But our toil he doth

sheds on our way! While we do his good will, He a-bides with us
drives it a-way; Not a doubt nor a fear, Not a sigh nor a
rich-ly re-pay; Not a grief nor a loss, Not a frown nor a

CHORUS.

still, And with all who will trust and o-bey. Trust and o-bey, For there's
tear Can a-bide while we trust and o-bey.
cross, But is blest if we trust and o-bey.

no oth-er way To be hap-py in Je-sus But to trust and o-bey.

4 But we never can prove
The delights of his love
Until all on the altar we lay,
For the favor he shows,
And the joy he bestows,
Are for all who will trust and obey.

6 Then in fellowship sweet
We will sit at his feet.
Or we'll walk by his side in the way;
What he says we will do,
Where he sends we will go,
Never fear, only trust and obey

Copyright, 1887, by D. B. Towner. Used by per.

172 Jesus will Give You Rest.

FANNY J CROSBY.   JNO. R. SWENEY.

1. Will you come, will you come, with your poor, broken heart, Burden'd and sin-op-
2. Will you come, will you come? there is mercy for you, Balm for your aching
3. Will you come, will you come? you have nothing to pay; Jesus, who loves you
4. Will you come, will you come? how he pleads with you now! Fly to his loving

pressed? Lay it down at the feet of your Sa - viour and Lord,
breast; On - ly come as you are, and be - lieve on his name,
best, By his death on the cross purchased life for your soul,
breast; And what- ev - er your sin or your sor - row may be,

CHORUS.

Je - sus will give you rest. Oh, hap- py rest! sweet, happy rest!

Je - sus will give you rest, Oh! why won't you come in

happy rest,

sim - ple, trust - ing faith? Je - sus will give you rest.

From "Joy to the World," by per.

We'll Never Say Good By.

"We shall never say 'good by' in heaven."—The words of a dying Christian woman.

Mrs. E. W. Chapman.　　　　　　　　　　　　　　J. H. Tenney.

1. Our friends on earth we meet with pleasure, While swift the moments fly,
2. How joyful is the thought that lingers, When loved ones cross death's sea,
3. No parting words shall e'er be spoken In that bright land of flowers,

Yet ev-er comes the thought of sadness That we must say good by.
That when our la-bors here are end-ed, With them we'll ev-er be.
But songs of joy, and peace, and gladness, Shall ev-ermore be ours.

CHORUS.

We'll nev-er say good by in heaven, We'll never say good by, ...
good by,

Repeat Chorus pp

For in that land of joy and song We'll never say good by.

Copyright, 1889, by John J. Hood.

We are Singing On the Way.

L. H. EDMUNDS.　　　　　　　　　　　　CHAS. EDW. POLLOCK.

1. We are sing-ing on the way, To a blessed land of day, Where the
2. What though trials here we meet? Soon we'll walk the golden street, Where we'll
3. We are pressing on the way, Let us work, and watch, and pray, Winning

raptured hal-le-lu-jahs nev-er cease; Soon we'll see its shining towers,
look up-on the beau-ty of our King; Tears of sorrow here may flow,
stars to sparkle in our crowns of light; Let us tell the Saviour's love,

Fine.

Rest within its lovely bowers, In that Eden-land of ev-er-lasting peace.
But "hereafter we shall know," And redeeming love thro' endless ages sing.
Till he bids us come above, Where no shadow ever mars the radiance bright.

D.S.—glory we shall share, In the house of "many mansions," bright and fair.

CHORUS.

Blessed home!　　blessed home!　　In the house of "many
Blessed home!　　blessed home!

D.S.

mansions," bright and fair;　　For we'll be like Je-sus there, And his
bright and fair;

Copyright, 1891, by W. J. Kirkpatrick.

175 Leaning on the Everlasting Arms.

Rev. E. A. Hoffman.   A. J. Showalter.

1. What a fel-lowship, what a joy divine, Leaning on the ev - er -
2. Oh, how sweet to walk in this pilgrim way, Leaning on the ev - er -
3. What have I to dread, what have I to fear, Leaning on the ev - er -

last - ing arms; What a bless-ed-ness, What a peace is mine,
last - ing arms; Oh, how bright the path grows from day to day,
last - ing arms? I have bless-ed peace with my Lord so near,

REFRAIN.

Lean - ing on the ev - er - last - ing arms. Lean - ing,
Lean - ing on the ev - er - last - ing arms.
Lean - ing on the ev - er - last - ing arms. Lean - ing on Je - sus,

lean - ing, Safe and se-cure from all a - larms;
Lean - ing on Je - sus,

Lean - ing, lean - ing, Leaning on the ev - er - lasting arms.
Lean-ing on Je - sus, lean-ing on Je - sus,

By per. A. J. Showalter.

We Walk by Faith.

FANNY J. CROSBY.　　　　　　　　　　　　　　WM. J. KIRKPATRICK.

1. We walk by faith, . . . and oh, how sweet . . The flow'rs that
2. We walk by faith, . . . he wills it so, ... And marks the
3. We walk by faith, . . . di-vine-ly blest, . . . On him we
4. And thus by faith, . . . till life shall end, . . . We'll walk with

grow . . . beneath our feet, . . And fragrance breathe a-long the
path . . . that we should go ; . . And when at times . . . our sky is
lean, . . . in him we rest ; . . . The more we trust . . our Shepherd's
him, . . . our dearest Friend, . . Till safe we tread . . . . the fields of

way . . . That leads the soul . . . to end-less day. . . .
dim, . . . He gen-tly draws . . . us close to him. . . .
care, . . . The more his love . . . 'tis ours to share. . . .
light, . . . Where faith is lost . . . . in per-fect sight. . . .

CHORUS.　　　　　　　　　　　　　　　　　*express.*

We walk by faith, but not alone, Our Shepherd's tender voice we hear,

And feel his hand within our own, And know that he is al-ways near.

Copyright, 1885, by WM. J. KIRKPATRICK.　　153

The Gospel Feast.

CHARLES WESLEY.
Cho. by H. L. G.
"Come, for all things are ready."
Luke xiv. 16.
H. L. GILMOUR.

1. Come, sinners, to the gos-pel feast; It is for you, it is for me;
2. Ye need not one be left behind, It is for you, it is for me;

Let ev'-ry soul be Je-sus' guest: It is for you, it is for me.
For God hath bid-den all mankind, It is for you, it is for me.

Fine.

D.S.—O wea-ry wand'rer, come and see, It is for you, it is for me.

CHORUS.

Sal-va-tion full, sal-vation free, The price was paid on Calva-ry;

D.S.

3 Sent by my Lord, on you I call;
  The invitation is to all:

4 Come, all the world! come, sinner, thou!
  All things in Christ are ready now.

5 Come, all ye souls by sin oppressed,
  Ye restless wanderers after rest;

6 Ye poor, and maimed, and halt, and blind
  In Christ a hearty welcome find.

7 My message as from God receive;
  Ye all may come to Christ and live:

8 O let this love your hearts constrain,
  Nor suffer him to die in vain.

9 See him set forth before your eyes,
  That precious, bleeding sacrifice:

10 His offered benefits embrace,
   And freely now be saved by grace.

Copyright, 1899, by H. L. Gilmour.

178 He is Calling.

Arr. by S. J. VAIL.

1st. 2d.

1. {There's a wideness in God's mercy, Like the wideness of the sea:
   {There's a kindness in his justice Which is more than } li-berty.

He is call-ing, "Come to me!" Lord, I'll glad-iy haste to thee.

2 There is welcome for the sinner,
And more graces for the good ;
There is mercy with the Saviour;
There is healing in his blood.

3 For the love of God is broader
Than the measure of man's mind;

And the heart of the Eternal
Is most wonderful and kind.

4 If our love were but more simple,
We should take him at his word;
And our lives would be all sunshine
In the sweetness of our Lord.

179   Vale of Beulah.

E. A. HOFFMAN.

JOSEPH GARRISON.

1. { I am passing down the val - ley that they say is so long,
   { 'Tis to me the vale of Beu - lah, 'tis a beau - ti - ful way,

2. { Not a shad - ow, not a shad - ow ev - er dark - ens the way,
   { And the mu - sic, sweetly chanted by the heav - en - ly throng,

3. { So I journey with re-joic - ing toward the Cit - y of Light,
   { And I near the o - pen por - tals of the kingdom a - bove,

But I find that all the pathway is with flow'rs o - ver-grown ; }
For the Saviour walks be - side me, my compan - ion all day. }

For a radiance of rare glo - ry shines up - on it all day : }
Floats in ca - dence down the val - ley, and it cheers me a - long. }

While each day my joy is deep - er, and the path grows more bright ; }
For this highway leads to Ca - naan, to the Kingdom of Love. }

D.S.–For the love - ly land of Ca - naan in the dis - tance I see.

CHORUS.   D.S

Vale of Beulah! Vale of Beulah! Thou art precious to me;

Copyright, 1898, by E. A. Hoffman.

INDEX.

www.ingramcontent.com/pod-product-compliance
Lightning Source LLC
Chambersburg PA
CBHW020557270326
41927CB00006B/873

9 783337 266349